The Poe of
of
Mark Legge

Author ~ Mark Legge
Published by Mark Legge

*To Jack, Sam and Henry
with Fond Regards
Legge [?]*

"Thy ink flows free
to engage thee
in rhyme,
valid or squib.
So let there be not one amongst who seeks to
guide direction,
hamper rampant progress,
or reduce resonant volume
or the impact
of thy nib."

i

"May I extend,
a thankyou to resilience.
For in times of perplexity
there is no better friend"

This first edition published 2007.
Published and bound in Great Britain.

ISBN 978 0 9555206 0 0

ii

Contents

If Only

I came upon the wishing well
sculpted from stony sand.
Its antiquated features lay
beneath neglected land.
Swirling barbs of blackberry and nettles virgin sting,
sought to prevent access
to any living thing,
for nature had created a repulsing interlace,
attempts by kindred mother to conceal this wretched place,
if only such resistance
had always been the case.

Forcefully my steps retrace the route trodden by seed,
clutching claws, rip at flesh and willingly I bleed,
bubbling blisters multiply upon my exposed frame,
but carcass numbed by torture
feels no external pain,
for stab and laceration are so scant a price to pay,
a just reward for negligence,
a child allowed to stray.

Finally I reach the place, its abyss is no more,
capped by layers of concrete so no other shall explore.
A tiny hole for drainage is the only access now,
a steady stream of saline
is all the grief it will allow,
interspersed with dripping blood
they filter through secreting ground
down to the sacred quench below
where part of me was found.

"If only...", is my wish.

Tempting Trips

"ROLL UP, ROLL UP, STEP THIS WAY,
EXCURSIONS LASTING JUST ONE DAY,
HAVE YOUR AFTERLIFE UNFURLED,
WITH A TRIP INTO THE SPIRIT WORLD.
The mornings spent in heavens heights,
taking in celestial sights,
after noon we'll drop and dwell
into the fiery depths of hell.
DON'T MISS THIS CHANCE FOLKS, DON'T DELAY,
ROLL UP, ROLL UP, STEP THIS WAY,
a unique window to decide,
which pathway to the other side".

Intrigue gripped the gathering crowd,
many, whom at first were cowed,
but as the show grew in allure,
the audience swelled by the score.
[There were those attracted by the glitz
and those restrained by cautious wits,
but ceaseless entice proved too great
for those that wished to pre-empt fate.]
Steadily the trickle streamed,
embarking on what they all deemed
an opportunity to see,
upon their death, how life would be.

"SHOWTIME"
with capacity reached, the void between the worlds was breached.
Transcending through all time and space
they came upon a hallowed place
where waiting guides with folded wings
harped a tune from rigid strings,
and so the flock was led to where
it caught a glimpse of Heavens stair,
ascending up and out of sight
through clouds immersed in brilliant light.

The mortal moths hypnotic state
drew them to a barring gate.
Pearly?
No, just to prevent
any kind of limbed ascent.
Upon it hung a helpful sign,
its content dealt with the incline.
ALAS THROUGH CONSTANT OVER USE
WE'VE HAD TO CLOSE THE TRADITIONAL ROUTE,
ONGOING WORK IS UNDERWAY
TO MINIMISE PROLONGED DELAY,
BUT TO ALLAY YOUR DISCONTENT,
WE'VE BUILT A LIFT FOR YOUR ASCENT.
No sooner had the words been read,
a lift appeared, as it had said.
All shuffled in with sheer delight,
confining doors then slid, sealed tight.
The automatic downward course
did not incite undue recourse,
until the heat began to soar
and beads evolved from every pore,
then suddenly the descent died,
secure doors split open wide.
The visitors recoiled in shock,
[met by flame and molten rock]
as from the depths of fiery core,
Lucifer stepped to the fore.
Eyes of blood and sinful stance,
he basked in ardent eminence,
then raising an extended claw,
he gently started to implore.
"Come my imps, don't be dismayed,
there is no need to be afraid,
as soon as you have paid my toll,
then you may leave,
WITHOUT YOUR SOUL ".

What's on the menu tonight ?

Must block out the icy cold,
shiver, shiver,
"Sir, if I may be so bold ",
shiver, shiver,
"have you got some change to lend,
or notes that you don't need to spend,
food and drink is all I seek,
I haven't eaten for a week!".

The stranger chooses to ignore
the craving tone of my implore.
Indignant strut upon his way,
oblivious to my dismay
and as the night does slowly fall,
hunger gnaws on stomach wall.
"I really don't know how much more of this that I can take".

I sit down on the freezing stone,
shiver, shiver,
contemplate my life alone,
shiver, shiver,
how is it I came to be
immersed in abject misery?
meandering upon the earth,
resigned to functions of no worth,
dependent now, indefinitely,
upon fragmented charity.
They say that it begins at home, that's true if you have one!

Across the street, the beef and fries,
shiver, shiver,
are wrapped in succulent disguise,
shiver, shiver.

I'd give anything to taste
portions of the bovine paste,
I know it's carrion of cow,
not a crucial fact right now,
perhaps! it is, that I can find
remnants in the waste behind,
I creep to destination, salvation is at hand.

The metal sticks to numbing skin,
shiver, shiver,
"**Curse** this **Greedy, Rotten** bin,"
shiver, shiver.
A plank of wood, a thrusting clip,
the lid bursts from its glacial grip,
I can not reach, what is in there?
a kindred trolley forms a stair,
instantly I retch and wrench
afflicted by the putrid stench,
but when you've nothing left inside there's little you can lose.

I wilt amidst the mental mire,
shiver, shiver,
exertions force me to tire,
shiver, shiver.
Weighted eyelids slowly sink,
senses teeter on the brink,
these crumpled empty boxes might
just prove to be welcome respite.
Perhaps I'll find some peace in rest, whilst
buried in this cardboard nest.
I feel as if I could sleep forever,

perhaps tonight I will?

Taken for a ride

"So it's me!"
who is on trial and standing in the dock,
suffering this barrage as his lawyer runs amok.
Portrayed as a prostitute by lashing legal tongue,
"WHY'S IT ME UNDER ATTACK? IT'S HE THAT DID THE WRONG!"

The onslaught is incessant and bombardment takes its toll,
battered to confusion, the repressed tears begin to roll,
finally I crumple, magnifying my mistake,
of thinking that a gentlemen had took me on a date.

The trial proceeded on it's course, the jury came to see,
umpteen testimonials of an unblemished history
and so initial empathy that was with the abused,
levelled, then subsided, till it came to rest with the accused.
Summing up the court was cleared, then refilled to decide,
in favour of the monster,
the judge then freed the man that lied.
Joyous hugs,
backs were slapped
to celebrate rules that were scrapped,
my strength was weak, but injustice then forced me to adapt.
I scrutinised with acute eyes the movements that he made,
as he enjoyed the plaudits of his innocent charade.
He turned to me, though fleetingly,
with gloating smirk of victory,
little did he know what I'd possessed with sectioned key.
All hands were shook, he turned away,
diminishing from the display,
but as he left he noticed not that neither did I stay.
I followed him out through the doors,
his mind distracted by applause
did wander, as did he, in his attempts to find relief.

Yet again we are alone as his fluid drains,
this time it's his bladder and wont leave ejaculating stains,
he gleams content, with legs apart, just as when we last met,
only then, it was mine forced, the night I can't forget.
But hurry, clear distracting thoughts, the deeds still to be done,
now it's me to take the lead and revel in the fun.

The concealed cloth of chloroform was taken from it's place,
mounting,
I clung like a leech
until a glaze possessed his face.
Then excreting the scalpel knife,
you may well think me crackers?
I set about incisively parting him from his knackers.
The act was swift,
I'm glad that he could smile through the event,
for so did I,
now that I,
had unloaded his instrument
and now perhaps in future,
instead of wanton lust,
this surgery
will hopefully have cured his urge to rip and thrust.

I'd not found inner resolve,
to show this animal ruth,
but unlike him, I did not seek concealment of the truth.
Arrested. Incarcerated. Investigated. Then to trial,
throughout I imitated him and acted for the while.
Performing for psychologists meant technicality,
persuaded judge of state and she allowed me to go free.

Now turning to the villain as I'm released by the clerk.
As a parting gesture, I return the victor's smirk.

7

Anyone for tea?

"Well then Captain Maritime, how do you like your tea?
Milk?, cream?, sugar?, lumps?, one?, two?, or three?"

"I don't partake of sweetness, but your cream looks rather lush,
the textures richly rigid, I'm not that keen on runny slush".

Miss Himplehorn infused the leaves
then scooped from relevant pots,
arriving at the guests cup,
she added several clots.
Then inserting a teaspoon, she moved as if to stir,

"Dear Lady please leave it to float, it is as I prefer".

Taking cup to mouth his smallest finger did protrude,
he slowly sipped and then exclaimed
"the flavours somewhat crude!",
swishing round his mouth,
"you know I can't quite place the taste,
I'm sure I've sampled such before",
he gulped the rest with haste.
As the last was swallowed, some cream sat upon his lip,
wiping off the residue, his thoughts re-turned to seamanship.

"In all the years upon the waves in harbours near and far,
I can't remember sampling a better cup of char.
Which breed of cow produced it?, for savour does not fade",

"just wait I'll ring for Dizzy, our most recent dairy maid".

Knock, knock, "come in, ah Dizzy,
what kind of breed is Bess?,
our visitor commends the cream, he praises too excess".

"Beggin yur pardon Madam, but this morn old Bess was dry,
so I shifted stool te next stall,
te give the newest cow a try.
At first she seemed reluctant, so I fumbled and I stroked,
a swollen teat slid to my hand, hardened it proudly poked.
The cow then seemed to relax, so I set about my chore,
I caressed, same as I'd been taught, but still it wouldn't draw.
At first I thought, she too, was dry, then came a sudden flow,
there was no milk, just oozing cream, so then I looked below.
She really is the strangest cow, she only has one udder",
her telling words, though innocent
made those assembled shudder.

"Oh Dizzy May, for goodness sake, you really are so dull,
the beast next door to Old Bess is our newly purchased bull!"

Splutter.

The Cuddlehog

Dejectedly it glares at me, its beady eye draws empathy,
laid upon its side with all four trotters tethered tight.
Long since has the struggle ceased
to rid itself of roped restraint,
but urge, though dissipated, festers patiently.
There is the odd spasmodic twitch
as I apply the globs of grease,
domesticated fat of geese,
little does it know it will prolong its piggish life,
though only fleetingly.
For as it slips, dips, slides and swerves
seeking the freedom it deserves,
those sturdy legs will start to tire
from long pursuit amidst the mire,
then succumbing to capture,
the turning spit awaits.

Hurriedly I turn it, smothering the other side,
hoping that the increased layers
will somehow give at least a chance,
then when the prize is won I'll know I did my best for it.
It! It! It deserves much more than that,
at least a fitting name.
Come now let me see.

Squeal? Reel? Wriggle? Die?
Chop? Hock? Ham? Pie?
Sizzle? Fizzle? Crackle? Fry?
No none of these seem apt, what if I call him pore?
it describes the way he eye's me and his chances of escape.
I think I'll stick with Pig.
Simple and detached.
Just then the cover opens, sunlight streams into the tent,
the beam of light though from above, is not heaven sent,
it is no ray of hope.

We're eclipsed by the hogger who's come to collect the swine,
placing knee onto Pigs side he neatly slits the twine.
Then holding hocks, ignoring squeals
he stretches out the slack,
with swooping swing around his neck, the pork is on his back,
"thanking you Nathaniel", is acknowledgement for my share,
suddenly the imminent departures hard to bare.
'Slit' steps through the exit, both pig and canvass flap,
I shuffle out, see struggle, see Pigs inclination sap,
nodding with the rhythmic step, as if consigned to fate,
he seems to understand he'll soon be basted on a plate.
I can not watch, I have to leave, get anywhere from here,
I just can't bare the thought of him rotated on a spear.
But wait! what kind of man am I despite my thirteen years,
to leave poor Pig abandoned, to face pursuing fears.
No, I will not do it! for whether boy or man,
I must conceive and then perform a piglet preservation plan.
But what on earth can I do?, he is as good as cooked,
cummon now think, think, think, what's been overlooked?

No there's nothing can be done!
My head and mood are bowed,
Forlorn, I stand and slowly fade,
become immersed within the crowd.

"Coooodullhooooooog".

Traditions call, beckons all, a violin begins to play,
groups of gathering folk prepare to dance the 'Southern way'.

[For Cuddlehog music sheet, proceed to page 164]

Doodle, da da, doodle da da, dum dum dum,
doodle, da da, doodle da da, dum dum dum,
doodle, da da, doodle da da , dum dum dee,
dee, dum dum, doodle, da da, dum dum, dee.

"Take yur pardners by the hand,
twirl those belles on Southern land,
chasing swine in a muddy bog,
cummon let's do, 'The Cuddlehog".

(instrumental)

"Grab yur hog and hold her tight,
she wriggles free and takes to flight,
left covered in a greasy glob,
ain't easy to cuddle a hog".

(instrumental)

"Don't give in, take up the chase,
slippin and slidin all over the place,
to pin her down will be a slog,
have you the wits to catch yur hog".

(instrumental)

"She's tiring now proceed with haste,
leap and grab her round the waist,
root her down as if a log,
what's it like to cuddle yur hog".

(instrumental)

"Now she is no longer free,
parade yur hog for all to see,
the covetous all stand agog,
wishin they could cuddle yur hog".

Doodle, da da, doodle da da, dum dum dum,
doodle, da da, doodle, da da, dum dum dum,
doodle, da da, doodle, da da, dum dum, dee,
dee, dum dum, diddle, eye, dow.

Dancing slowly peters out, though momentarily,
as prancing round the stacks
will recommence after the following spree.
Expectant voices chatter, anticipation's on the rise,
for who from those assembled,
will squeeze and win the scampering prize.

Whoops, shouts, shrieks and hollering,
greet then quickly cease,
on arrival of that coveted,
all ready for release.
But first, an ancient customary needs to be observed,
the redneck and his rituals must always be preserved.
For rules laid down by ancestry decreed that every man,
shall shuffle to position, rotate, create an arms lengths span.
[This mass of twirling fuddled folk makes an amusing sight,
its aim is respect for the hog, to make space for its flight,
(it also mimics how the beast will roast later that night)].

"spread to spot and spin".

There's hustle and there's bustle as opponents interact,
when partial paralytics pirouette there'll always be contact,
with clips, trips, slaps, whacks, bumps, thumps, cuffs from
whisky'd one and all,
it meant esteemed occasion soon descended to a brawl.
Bodies fluctuated in a conflicting ho-down,
punches rained incessantly for notoriety's fighting crown,
the congregated chorus escalated in its din,
until there came a loud impacting blast from concealed culverin.
[an antiquated weapon, its effect was none the less,
it brought mayhem to standstill, now the contest could progress]

With faces bruised and battered, but ego's still intact, consensus?
disappointment, that they'd had to end contact.

"spread to spot and spin".

Again came the instruction, this time it was a ruse,
for as they once again did swirl, the rapt pig was let loose.

Jittery jolts afflicted him, but he just could not construe
why all around were in a spin,
but not one did pursue,

"hogs away".

A raucous roar erupted,
which left Pig in no doubt,
for the nearest to him lunged
and firmly grasped him round the snout.
Squealing with indignity, snatching from the clutch,
brawny biceps beetled before others got a touch.
Dodging this and that way. Rotating on a dime.
Twisting, listing, duck or dive reactions are sublime,
around, up and over, through legs, he's a blur of dashing pink,
bodies stumble, fumble, fall as if upon a rink.
The pigs simply to nifty, competitors outclassed,
it doesn't matter what they fling, cus everything is passed.
Most chasing, snaking aimlessly, all following their lead,
have yet to get a sight of pig, let alone perform the deed.
[Nathaniel in amongst them, had no desire to chase,
all he could envisage was the spitting piglets face.
For whether soon or later, no matter what Pig tries,
the hounding hordes will hunt him down and that's the time he
dies!]

Some time later through exertions, the crowd begins to thin,
exhaustion, thirst or injury, subdued attempts to gin.

But also from his efforts,
amidst the limbed chicane,
Pig, though still perceptive, also began to wane.
[At this point in proceedings, fickle fate chose to transpire,
a fortunate encounter between two within the mire,
for Pig with sapping strength,
chose to turn his ebbing course,
directly at the young boy, who still tussled with remorse.]
I looked at Pig, Pig looked back,
then gaze was drawn to chasing pack,
I took to flight and soon we were both running side by side,
harmonious in stride,
conscious of predicament, four fearful eyes were opened wide
as several of the melee closed to within gripping grasp,
stretching hands,
reached and strained to clinch the telling clasp.
The nearest man exerted, overbalanced and then slipped,
falling to the ground his sprawling body accidentally clipped
my heels
which caused my legs to tangle and I crashed down to the floor,
the chasing huddle tumbled as
they reached the mound that lay afore,
creating groping hillock, a perplexed human pile,
[but to compound confusion, those arriving became infantile]
on seeing the predicament of those that had fallen,
they promptly jumped and built themselves
into a huge mountain of men.
The watching crowd all revelled in the heightening display,
though none had seemed to notice that
the prancing pig had gone astray,
efficient, safety marshals, took swift steps to intervene,
sensing crushing danger they were quickly on the scene.
Plucking, bucking, chucking, disassembling at pace,
crudely they dismantled the irregular embrace,
till finally they came upon the founding final tier,
the man who had first stumbled,
had made himself into a pier

and arched his body over mine as protection from plight,
as he slowly reared
the unexpected came to sight.
Beneath there was not one, but two that nestled in the bog,
there I lay,
proud as punch,
cuddling my hog.

"The Winner ".

A second roar erupted, items tossed into the air
and so began the hoe down, each in step to violin fanfare.
The Marshall went to raise my hand, it took him several tries,
for now that I had hold of him, I had no wish to loose the prize.
And so young boy and beast were elevated for a while,
I glanced at Pig and could have sworn
I saw the semblance of a smile.

But that was many years ago and now I'm an old man,
I smothered Pig with comfort till the end of his life span.
I even saved his bacon during the uncivil war,
I have so many memories of me and my 'Old Pore'.

I shall no longer reminisce, for now my eyes begin to fog,
this here is the story of my first and only 'Cuddlehog'.

This is an extract from
'The diaries of Nathaniel Peppercorn 1846 ~1947'

Did

Did you cast a roving eye that lured you to deceit?
did your carnal actions, then make you feel complete?
Did your thoughts not falter to discovered consequence?
was it worth the pleasure now your family fragments?
Did you think that I would just except your selfish ways?
whilst other lusting laddish clones all showered you with praise?

Did you take me for a fool,
did you break the crucial rule,
did you take me by the hand,
did you place the golden band,
did you pledge eternal love until the bitter end?

well did you, did you, did yOU, DID OR DIDN'T YOU?

Suspended

Roughened rope that's neatly twined is looped around, ready to bind,
then apple gulps upon the chime
as all too soon,

"It is time".

Led along the lonely path no other soul would want to tread,
placed above the purging flaps that descend to the dead.
Grip of steel then knuckles white
to execute the parasite,
but calculations through the deck,
inadequately snap the neck.
Intended end does not occur,
this failure becomes the spur,
that jolts the condemned back to life,
salvations surge becomes his knife,
which reaches up to cut the string,
then freedoms fall is abiding.

This vision is but vagary, and that sentenced, is left to swing,
kicking, puking, wriggling,
heavy limbs draw gasps for breath,
repulse, convulse, fight to the death,
constricting fibres will not stop,
as taught contraction from the drop
does slowly drain what's left of life,

flail, fumble, fail,
ail,
flail, fumble, fail,
ail,

18

violent tugs, resisting turns,
but no one slips the tie that burns.
Determined dance does slowly wane,
his final words become profane,
then blue imbues the stricken tongue,
the struggles lost,
the beast is hung.

After the frantic jerking battle,
comes the gurgling death rattle,
swinging limply from the frame,
he only has himself to blame.

Protect the decent, guard their fate,
apply the noose,
ERADICATE.

Deposit then Depose

"God damn it General Warmonger your notion is absurd,
do you seriously expect me to except we've been struck,
by a turd!?,
It almost wiped out Utah after plummeting from space,
God knows how many polygamists were lost without a trace?
Are you part of a conspiracy to label me a twit?
would you have me tell America,
the projectile was a giant shit?"

"If yull allow me Mr President, analysis is clear.
We've scrutinised the meteorite for well over a year.
Considering economy
we started with astronomy
then experts in petrology, geology, scatology
examined the whole sight with a meticulous toothed comb,
no rock was left unturned as we inspected the inverted dome.
The crater had us baffled till
'it' surfaced at the core,
in amongst the debris we unearthed a microscopic spore.
Back at the laboratory, geneticists did find,
D.N.A, which it transpires was of the human kind.
Processing information to awaiting data bank,
instantly it came up with a number, name and rank.
Alexander Kremlinitch a Russian cosmonaut
must have ejected his excrement through an external port.
Cast out to infinity the mess did not comply,
instead of degradation, the little shit did multiply,
festering reaction became putrefying slick,
glutinous in texture, all it touched did ultimately stick
creating the expansion for trajected final course,
perhaps the rampant microbes sought discovery of source?"

"I scarcely can believe my ears, it sounds out of this world,
who could possibly have then foreseen
the consequence that you've unfurled.

But to implicate the Soviets would break beyond repair,
an unstable alliance, it would mean political nightmare!
this impact must not swell to where two continents collide,
I WILL NOT engage acts that lead to presidential suicide".

"Perhaps I can alleviate apocalyptic fear!
To avoid altercation, we will have to volunteer,
a slight elaboration of the facts we have to hand,
we merely need to shift the course of blame
just slightly overland".

The presider's mood mutated, twinkled intrigue lit his eye,
"against which other nation will you cultivate the lie?"

"I've graded groups of oil and yield and made a relevant list.
Removed all those possessing the ability to resist.
Set this against all astronauts who've left our atmosphere,
one of them is from the required region of the sphere".

"Excellent.
You'll get your share,
but come now let's make haste,
amend the files, prepare missiles there is no time to waste.
Then call the press and broadcasters so that we may confirm,
a war of retribution!

That should secure another term".

Goodbye

A single tear.
No more,
no less,
is all I will allow.
Sorrow's surge will know its place, resolve WILL retain my grief.

This porous heart absorbs the pain of wasted years,
shattered dreams,
yearning for some common ground, but we never could agree.
Stubborn traits, too similar,
opened wounds that never healed,
divide afflicted by an age.

Now of course it is too late, the toll of life becomes a knell,
death has come to taint the lives
of those that mourn a passing life.
I stand above unsettled earth, your casket waits in readiness,
bending down I place a coin, upon the polished coffin lid,
it is the one that we once found whilst rummaging
when I was young.
Sliding tips, sense the grain, that pines above your heart,
I pause before I weigh it down
with clumps of soil that come to hand.
Thoughts drift ahead,
length unknown, to when this barrier does decay,
forcing the said penny to drop, to a place where I once was.
Perhaps it's then and only then
that you will come to understand,
persistence of futility,
only leads to misery and thoughts of that
which could have been.

Life's too short and deaths too long.

As mists disperse and thoughts resume,
to the current time and place,
troubled soil returns to where, it can settle as before.
You are slowly sprinkled, forever from my sight,
then it dawns,
as the son,
that I will not see you again.
That lonely tear,
so resolute,
becomes the prelude to a stream,
which cascades down my crumpled face,
to join your final resting place.
The soil is cleansed, my soul is purged,
the torment rushes from within,
the sudden impact of release has come to make me realise.

Hands of time will not rewind for troubled, you or I,
the tide of yet another life has ebbed and flowed away.

All I know is what I feel.

I love you Dad,
I always have
and I always will,
and somehow,
though it is too late,
I know you loved me too.

Upstanding members of the cast

Mine is a tortured soul.
Stretched by time and consequence,
racked by distant memories that seem as yesterday.
Regression holds the key.
Access to release.
But the bunch is copious,
with each and all, catalysts as I recall,
implements to corridors to abuse and beyond.
Let's search and jangle purposely.

"Take me back."

Darkness greets awakening,
levitation in a void,
it's black as pitch
nothing stirs, I can not see though eyes are wide
or are they sealed?
fingers fail to ascertain as absent limbs are impotent.
What is this place?

I do not breath, but am not dead,
this comprehension brings no fear,
emotion does not reside here,
nothing seems to reside here,
is this the final resting place where tortured souls remain?
Wait. Listen.........?
Clankings sound
though feint at first, rattles, battles barriers,
beguiling revolutions delve to cleave malignancy.
Revelations nick and notch,
sexagonal holes, blink shafts of light,
piercing shards dissect the gloom
to incise brittle core,
evoking squints of that before.

One by one extinguished rays relight from failure,
then that locked slowly returns.
Suddenly I'm sucked then spewed
into surroundings recognised,
it is the room,
the Theatre
where indecent acts were staged,
still dark and dank and desolate,
cept for flickering candlelight, which suffices for lime.
Way back then I had the lead
all eyes and lewd activity were focused and performed on me,
with passions roused,
actors acted fervently
caressing parts incessantly
taking turns to enter their portrayal of the role,
me a filthy puppet, satisfaction for their strings.

But now I'm back.
I've come to know that life has passed,
I've learned how to direct and I'm dispensing with the cast.
I'm bringing down the curtain on this lingering foul play,
the players and their audience shall be ushered away.
For those that chose to probe
and then immerse themselves in bliss,
shall have no further prominent parts
this cast is reviewed
to abyss.

This wayward play is at an end.

"bring me back."

Closure is mine.

To those that like a flutter

Tell me.
What's the odds an elephant will fly in outer space,
or lasting peace will emanate throughout the human race?
Or what's the odds a conker having read of William's fight,
would presume itself noble and pursue title of knight?
What's the odds a blue baboon whilst crooning moonlit tune,
would grab hold of an old buffoon and dance the rigadoon?
Or what's the odds of atmosphere diminishing from sky?
or raging rivers receding until their ripples trickle dry?
or that one day we all will share the darkness of the blind?
or reparations time machine allows our ravage to rewind?

What's the odds that arrogance will never show contempt,
or odds of winning lottery at very first attempt?
Or what's the odds that mankind will see cooling of the sun,
before he sees total eradication of the gun?
Totalize,
talk to your tipsters, raise the stakes,
mull over mixtures,
have you worked out probability?
if so,
I have one more.

In countryside in Staffordshire out at a place called Fauld,
the year was nineteen forty four
and winters grasp had taken hold.
A man named Maurice Goodwin busily worked on his farm,
tending to his livestock to ensure that they came to no harm,
when suddenly a rumbling made all around him shake,
the earth beneath him shuddered, escalating to a quake.
Then a violent eruption with an impact, so severe,
it burst through the crust, rose up, then sank to leave
imploded hemisphere.

Farmer, farm, workers and all were sucked into the ground
and up until this very day no fragment has been found.

The reason for catastrophe?

Bombs stocked by the ministry in an old gypsum mine,
consequentially exploded,
perhaps from misguided woodbine.
Akin to Hiroshima but miles beneath the soil,
oblivious, all those above continuing with daily toil,
were blown up to the heavens,
then squashed flatter than a pat.
Now you who like to gamble
tell me,
what's the odds of THAT?

Rut

"Lick, lick, lick my arse, lick my arse for life",
the mandate stipulated to a subservient wife.
Daily drudged procession amidst mottled pot and pan,
acting on the impulse of a mollycoddled man.
Banquets dished on handed plates,
nothing he appreciates,
enduring repulsive traits,
scrubbing all he defecates.
Performing sole dictates,
exactly as he states,
whilst that which once was idyllic, slowly disintegrates.
I once did radiate,
now I'm inanimate,
a selfless acquiescent shell that panders to placate.

Prick, prick, prick my arse, prick my arse for life,
the submissive implosion of a prostituted wife.
Perverse postures performed at a rhythmic rota'd span,
acting on the impulse of a mollycoddled man.
Willingness is obligated,
passion must be consummated,
expected to titillate,
vibrate,
gyrate,
fabricate.
Manoeuvred manipulation,
onus on ejaculation,
reproducing violation.

Left alone prostrate,
to ponder melancholy state,
how much more of this life can my resolve tolerate?

Wricked, wricked, wricked and sparse, wricked and sparse for life,
resigned, benign acceptance by intimidated wife,
demanding, reprimanding scourge, just because he can,
chauvinistic imposition of a mollycoddled man.
Her thoughts dissolve in desolation,
escalating desperation,
craving those who can relate
to vegetating mental state.
Her fundamental reservations,
succumb to self preservation,
tears fall, fears form her oration,
blissful prescribed medication.

Emerging elation,
deflects the deflation,
arousing realisation.

Kick, kick, kick this farce, kick this farce for life,
the conclusion established by rejuvenated wife.
Surfacing rebellion, because, she simply can,
reacting to the impulse of a mollycoddled man.
Coercing communication,
releasing the remonstration,
finished with frustration,
this servant is no more.
Commenced consternation,
clenched intimidation,
hurled humiliation,
urges me to door.

Validating vindication,
energised emancipation,
liberating litigation.
I've earned every penny, now it's my time to explore.

Naturally

Mr Harold Horticulture,
renowned as a seasoned mulcher,
fingers greener than the fly
condemned to death on plants nearby,
has gardens that are floral shrines,
acids fuse with alkalines,
complementing hues and shades,
enthusiasm never fades.

Down 'Covert Close' he has a plot,
consumables!
he grows the lot.
Every contest he is in
ends with a decisive win,
rosettes, trophies, cups amassed
from produce as yet unsurpassed.

His secret? ah! now there's a tale
he once divulged whilst supping ale.
"Varying diet has made me wiser,
in me quest for fertiliser.
[whisper]The reasons behind my success. A bowel concocting perfect cess".

Seems Harold's a true Democrat,
his notion of to share is that
come spreading time the case is such,
he likes to add his personal touch.

It's now that I'd like to confide
he sells his 'turn out' countrywide,
so next time you are wined and dined
I'm sure your meal will be refined,
but whilst not wishing to be crude
it's only right that I include
consuming facts to be construed.
"You could be eating Harold's food!"

Inbred

9/11~13. Unlucky
for more than some.
Towering insanity which struck a nation dumb.
The latest in a list as long as length of distinct span,
the time in which the earth has been inhabited by man.
Manufactured homicide,
        genocide,
        foeticide.
        Germicide,
        vermicide,
        fungicide,
        lungicide.
        Insecticide,
        infecticide
        infanticide,
        giganticide. Continued executions, done overtly
or by stealth.

Finally comes suicide,
he even kills himself.

31

Who?

Who was the first man to evolve?
who was the first to cry?
who was the first to burst with joy?
who was the first to sigh?
Who was the first man to caress?
who was the first to see?
who was the first to sense a scent or hear the call of destiny?
Look upon reflection.
Are you that man?

Who was the first to take a step?
who was the first to stride?
who first succumbed to elements and either froze or fried?
Who rose to take the challenge then endeavoured to achieve?
Who ventured down to hidden depths then battled to upheave?
Who exerted to rupture or until they had no more?
who conquered tides of emotion to find another sure?
who first was drawn up to the skies, who was the first to fly?
who was the first to understand then reason as to why?
Reflect upon reflection.
Are you that man?

Who first did become envious?
who first yielded to greed?
who first took that which was not theirs
although they had no need?
Who first encountered anger?
who first encountered rage?
who was the first to lack restraint necessitating cage?
Who was the first man to conspire or to create divide?
who was the first to wage a war or execute some form of cide?
when inner voices beckoned, who answered to their call?
who was the first to tame that beast which resides within all?
Reflect on imperfection.
Are you that man?

Who was the first to create fire, or first to burn in hell?
who first created Heaven, who first became a shell?
Who first did speak the language, universal in appeal?
who was first to write or read or decide what was real?
Who was the first to question as to origin of man?
was he from the Pongidae or was he Biblican?
Who was first to sow that seed or cultivate that lie?
who first dispelled immortal myth?
Who was the first to die?
Reflect on resurrection.
Were you that man?

The Jolly Boatman

Chuck a chunk, chuck a chunk,
chuck a chunk, chuck a chunk,
chuck a chunk, chuck a chunk,
chuck a chunk, chuck a chunk,
chuck a chunk, chuck a chunk,
chuck a chunk, chuck a chunk,
chuck a chunk, chuck a chunk,
chuck a chunk, chuck a chunk,
chuck a chunk, chuck a chunk,
chuck a chunk, chuck a chunk,
chuck a chunk, chuck a chunk,
chuck a chunk, chuck a chunk,
chuck a chunk, chuck a chunk,
chuck a chunk.
Gliding to and from the slaughter
on manipulated water
leisurely he guides his barge,
perfect murderous camouflage.

Travelling miles between the earth
he seeks befitting place to berth,
[passing by he'll raise a hand with pleasantries exchanged,
he imitates a jolly man, facade of the deranged]
for friendly face and sunny smile
conceal intentions, to most, vile,
but veneer stays untarnished
till he finds a place to harness
then,
he waits.

Assisted by the lack of light,
he steps and merges with the night,
then treads a path invisible to naked you or I.
Meticulous, not one to rush
whilst nestled in concealing bush,
he'll cast a cold discerning eye
on all those females passing by,
unsuspecting and alone, will you be the one?

For should you stumble on his path
then be prepared for frenzied wrath,
this demon strikes with evil zest,
meteing out eternal rest.

Seize the victim, slit her throat,
bag it, lift, no time to gloat,
throw it, weight, it mustn't float,
then gasping gulps rise from the moat.

Decreasing rings, a final wave,
last trace of this watery grave.

Now desires are satisfied
the lust drains from unconscious eyes
and once again a silent route is trodden as before.
Reaching home he goes beneath,
his heightened state is only brief,
for come the dawn he must depart,
fulfilling undetected start.
Nought is left for those behind
as he chuck a chunks to find
a new place to eliminate
victim number twenty eight.

The Hunt
(to be read at a galloping pace).

We're off to find, pursue and grind then catch the wily fox,
he's been busy in the game reserves diminishing the stocks.
Setting off at crack of dawn, we'll search and find the scent,
then chase him till the cows come home, we simply can't relent.

Come now let's be candid, I'm sure you will agree,
the hounds now in attendance are the finest pedigree.
Employed for their persistence, in waging war of wits,
hungry for a conquest they will rip the prize to bits.

"Are all now assembled? then off we go".

Clip clopping down the high street,
whilst we're pouting our parade,
we cloak our lust for blood beneath a pestilence charade,
passing through spectators, the dapper suits in tow,
sit upright in the saddle looking down on those below.
Certain city migrants, grimace with dismay,
as we reach the edge, go through the hedge,
the hunt is underway,

"Tally Ho".

Advancing into countryside, harrowing the turf,
obstacles are mastered as we roam upon the earth.
Hawthorn, gates and protesters encountered on our ride,
are assessed instantaneously and taken in our stride.
It's so exhilarating to be chasing in the hunt,
discovery's seduction, allures you to the front,
feel the chill that surges, creating nostril flare,
fresh and unpolluted it's invigorating air.

36

Galloping majestically to chorus of the hounds,
covering vast acreage with measured leaps and bounds,
first we're going this way, then we're going that,
we have approximation to exactly where he's at,
but just as we are warming up, pursuit comes to a halt,
fox's clever strategies the underlying fault.

Whilst canines are indulging in their frenzied foraging,
we take a welcome respite from the intense following,
criss-crossing energetically, scouring the moss,
purpose seems to dissipate, the pack are at a loss.
["You see.
The things that are required for this endeavour to succeed,
are endurance, adrenaline, and a trusted steed,
oh you must excuse me, forgive my paradox,
it's essentially significant to also have a fox.
ARTIFICIAL SCENTING!, perish such a thought,
surely you can understand, it simply isn't sport.
Look I haven't got the time for you to remonstrate,
it's bad enough we've lost the scent and have to sit and wait".]
Could it be the blighter, has given us the slip,
as thoughts drift to renewed attempts the bugler lets rip.

"**Tally Ho**".

There's the ruddy rascal with his bushy taunting tail,
he's heading for the sanctuary, that's in the yonder dale,
a labyrinth of warrens, which registers a doubt,
for should it be he gets there we will never get him out.

"Come along, drive them hard,
spur them on,
SPUR".

Reaching the horizon, no longer is he eyed,
but the hunt is in its full and awe inspiring stride,
enthusiastically we sprint up over turned and furrowed field,
destiny's determined that his final fate is sealed,
but as we burst over the slope imagine our dismay,
a fence that wasn't there has been erected in the way.

Completely unexpected,
the hounds are unaffected,
but as for those astride another story is to tell.
Those seasoned in the chase,
advanced and jumped at pace,
but those approaching gingerly, unfortunately fell.
Undeterred by incident, etiquette's maintained,
it's insignificant how any injuries obtained,
the minimum necessity we crucially require,
is dogged perseverance through whatever should transpire,
Leaving those that flounder, immerse yourself in thrill,
we're reaching point of closure and converging for the kill.

"Tally Ho".

You can predict with credence
now they're snapping at his heels,
that he has ate the last of any game or poultry meals.
With rampant breath and failing strength
they're ready to expunge,
nipping at his flagging flesh, he takes a final lunge,
straight into an awaiting hole, alas it is too late,
the hounds are promptly merciless,
they grasp and seal his fate.

As we arrive there's blood and guts and pieces everywhere,
but as we wade amongst them we find remnants of a hare.
The unsuspecting leveret, it seems, was rather rash,
awakened by the fox, his inbred instinct was to dash.
Normally his antics would have led a merry dance,
but with opened jaws assembled,
he never stood a chance.

Now the fox has gone to ground, he'll soon be up and running,
so tell me was he lucky, or is he simply cunning.

Saving Saviour

My mental state had lapsed into a mind consuming fog,
in need of instant contentment I sought to find a god.
Finally I found him after he had gone astray,
this blessed individual will be the one who leads the way.
Embracing his presence, I shall shower him with praise,
my faith in hymn will be the spur that sees my spirit raise
for he's opened up those avenues that I had feared to tread
and with him I now undertake to share my daily bread.
Yes, through this resurrection, he has been the driving cog,
no, I could not bare life without me and my devoted god.*

* Please excuse an error during publication,
  text corrections are as follows.
  god should read **dog** and **hymn** should read **him**.
  I must apologise for your ongoing confusion.**

** Please excuse an error during re-publication,
   text correction on the passage notifying re-corrections
   are as follows.
   your should read **the**.

Why?

Blip..blip..blip..blip
drip..drip..drip..drip

my eye's release their pent distress
as I survey the motionless
profile of my only child,
body recently defiled,
dissections from a surgeons knife,
attempts to preserve precious life,

blip..blip..blip..blip

intrusive lengths of wires and tubes
fed by pulsing medical cubes,
machinery Doctors implanted,
performing functions took for granted,

blip..blip..blip..blip

consumed within parental hell,
I am but a hollow shell,
knowing not what fate holds nigh,
could it be that she will die?
this can't be right!
she's done no wrong,
she's lived no life,
she is too young,
why is it death has been enticed?
why must she be sacrificed?
"damn you Lord", answer, impart,
the reasons why you crush my heart,
if filling quota's for the dead,
then re-arrange, take me instead,
for mine will be no life on earth,
without this child, nurtured from birth,

blip..blip..blip..blip..bleeeeeeeeeeeeeeep.

Cycling

Penelope Farthing the local bike
used to ride ten times a night,
except in winter when the frosty air
had pimples goosing everywhere.

[Not that it would stop her heaven,
it just reduced it down to seven.]

Churchyard, building, meadow, wood,
obliging men wherever she could,
until one day when on the job
whilst rogering a bloke named Bob
her feelings they began to swoon,
it ended that she came too soon.
The gentleman was not demanding,
instead he possessed understanding
and now he's become much more than,
just another cycling fan.
For they've upgraded the local bike,
she's now become a respectable trike
with baby Bob born yesterday,

she no longer rides that way.

Serenity

The young brunette surveyed the scene
way down below seemed so serene
and as it strengthened in allure, she teetered on the edge.

A gentle breeze, with soft caress
distracted briefly her distress
to lift her from impending plight
cajole her from attempted flight,
but feelings numbed by constant pain surfaced from deep within.

Again her lids released their swell
heaped memories of living hell
of swooning heart, ecstatic bliss, rejecting insult, then to this
for was she ever more to him
than meeting, conquest, single whim,
an object for his lurid lust,
receptacle for rampant thrust and as a notch upon his post,
carved,
then cast aside.

Her mood resumes worse than before,
emotions that can take no more.
Looking down at that beneath,
the blooming crowns and dappled heath
where Summers grasp had ousted Spring
and flora now changed everything.
Consuming thoughts became so clear,
calmness overcame the fear and vented anger waned.

"Goodbye to all those that remain,
you're welcome to your mortal pain".

Then drawing in her deepest breath, she stepped to an untimely
death.
A leap of faith had set her free,
now she has found
serenity.

Misdirected Nourishment

Purse your lips it's now innate
then suck the nipple of the state,
milk the goodness that is there,
abuse a system formed to care
for those that possess genuine need,
it wasn't built for idle greed.

So if from these shores or afar,
scroungers you know who you are,
lose your suckling repute,
prove your worth,
contribute.

**"I remember,
as if it were yesterday."
Am I the only one?**

Whistling,
the missiles rise
then shower as if rain.
Blistering explosions burst, again, **A**gain, **AGAIN**.
Helpless hollow hands attempt to stem the pound upon each drum,
"**CAN SOMEONE GET ME OUT OF HERE**",
I need to find sanctum.
End this momentum.
Flee these, deranged, ambitious waves which seek imperium.

Desperation's call does climb to fall upon deaf ears.
[I am but a pawn, a token, played to death by absent peers]
It makes no difference how I plead, the fighting does not cease,
this manufactured war endures, until
such time as we make peace.
Securing world's release,
whilst millions of saviours descend to their decease.

Isolated,
all alone,
accustomed to deaths stench.
Friendships lie fragmented,
dispersed, dislocated,
mangled, mutilated,
lives which were so vivid, decay, slayed within this sodden trench.
[An ebullient excavation, became burrows for the brave,
oblivious their furrowing was digging of their grave]
These recent recollections surge and pain swells to a blur.
Its haze is irresistible,
escape is its consuming lure,
eager to be absent,
I willingly concur.........

Delusion's sift
does slowly drift
away from mire that I am in.
The surreal quells
the shocking shells,
tumult fades to distant din.
Taint falls faint beyond me.
"I'm on my way back home!"
Across the sea,
to 'Old Blighty',
an island small,
but still mighty,
though currently imperilled,
she shall be forever free.
Up over,
cliffs of Dover, soaring through unfettered air,
obliging crow,
spits fire below,
bringing me to where.

Ashen smoke of oak rises from rustic chimney pots,
stacked upon a roof which rakes to brick once laid by eye.
Carefully assorted ends, meander, pave the way,
through rows of roses,
vibrant red,
shire fed, in regimented pristine bed,
avenues to ivy, arching over welcomes door,
forever on the latch.
A gentle push, tired hinges flag to judder with the floor,
established is the greeting, from tiles chequered with history.
Instant warmth coerces me to flicker of the flames,
flowing from cindered source,
lapping at lethargic logs
till prompt comes from bellow.

[Persistent nudging pokes arouse a simmering within.
Suddenly, that settled, rises to become inflamed,
summoning saps for spitting spats,
each aimed at dousing raging cause of he who is to blame]
Now embers glow to surging soar
which leaps up to dangled decor
to dance upon beloved brass,
each buffed to brilliance,
till lustre has attained,
reflections of an age.

Another log is thrown, to reinforce those gone before,
burning thoughts are drawn from those to those that I adore.
Smells once still familiar force famished feet to rove,
into awaiting kitchen, where Mother toils at labouring stove.
Rubicund, glistening, engrossed in roast of Sunday's breast,
devoted dedication, in her I'm truly blessed.
Intuition perceives presence, raise begets uplifting smile,
I study cherished features to then savour passing while.
Embracing warmth that follows is so good I can't let go.
Why did I leave this peaceful life, do I really know?
["Yes, of course, I do know,
I answered to the call,
to fight for King and country, keeping freedom for us all,
but millions dead, dying and wounded,
will be total sum.
This generations sacrifice
for all those yet to come"]

Out through distorted window pane, father tends the soil,
progressive germination forms integral part of daily toil.
As I reach to greet him,
he bids a fond farewell.
His grip of steel diminishes
as I'm propelled as if a shell,

as fingers,
clinging to the past
are ripped away from secure grasp
which flourishes into a proud, but fading final wave,
dwindling on doorstep of my idyllic enclave.
Drawn back passed the stacks of hay where memories were laid,
a summers kiss, grazing grass, the ploughman's lunch,
fresh lemonade!,
landing before Bromley, where the ancient Abbots prayed
and Dancers prance the Horned Parade,
long main street, lined with fortitude, no German shall subdue,
a vibrant vein which pulses patriotic red, white and blue.
Selected friends appear, to become slapped through crowded craze,
acknowledged by the masses,
enthralled by celebrations phase
passed Bloor the Blacksmith, glowing
whilst employing forged resources,
shodding
nodding horses,
beyond the fabled Buttercross,
[historical preserve]
Tommies on the way to give the Hun what he'll deserve.

As faces etched with hope and faith emerge from every glance,
fears of that, as yet unknown, are repressed by the jubilance,
the village band's melodic march begins to instrument its pride,
raw, aroused, ungainly steps, shift to regimented stride,
which troop's long rural arteries to pour from coastal docks,
uncertain waves are crossed amidst the pendulum hammocks,
ticking anxious time away,
toward our unknown end,
bolstered by the spirit of the British we defend.
We're called up to the writhing deck and imminent array,
thrust into the turmoil
we're showered by the hostile spray.........

Pitter-patters persist, prods and spatters me from trance,
though dull,
the droplets rise above the booms of bruising resonance
to drench the saturation, soaking overflowing pores,
feeding fungal hunger of accumulating spores.
But, there is no melancholy, from persistence of the rains,
natures tears will cleanse these carcasses of poppy stains.
Though incapacitation stops me stemming rodent feast,
they're gnawing ever nearer,
cessation won't be long,
at least.

Then from distant, cloaked obscurity, elegance arrives,
a Celtic dancer, skips, revolves, rejuvenates diminished lives
as one by one, she stops to tend, extend compassions hand,
resurrected from the cause, they emanate to stand.
Simple apparitions, essence pure as time before
their zest was drawn to defend in this devastating war.

"Go my friends, climb embankments,
  take your chance to leave this slough,
  enact with faith, your final push.
  The blisters can not burst you now".

Her movements irresistible, she skims across quagmire,
her captivating curlicue coerces eyes to tire.
Ladened lids lapse lower, till they shield me from the gore,
release is overwhelming.
I just can't live here anymore!

I know not name of angel who endeavoured to engage.
I know that her resilience enabled life till ripe old age.
I'm sitting in my wheelchair, decorated for 'the day',
I Remember,
but I see that other memories have gone astray.
Forgotten are those heroes, who fought and gave their life,
forgotten is the sacrifice and pain that was so rife.
Forgotten are the deeds that went beyond expectancy,
so you could live your current lives and be totally free.
Now, all I see is apathy
and so I write this rhyme,
it's aimed at those who can not spare two minutes of 'their' time.
Those renegers of the silence,
it's **YOU** that this is aimed
and for your utter disrespect you **SHOULD BE** damned
ASHAMED!

As a Mark of respect for those who've fought and lived or lost
their lives. There are 1111 words in this commemorative poem.

A Pirate's Tale

William Bantock is my name,
I've sailed the sea's to high acclaim.
Better known as 'Bloody Bill'
with my marauding motley crew
we steal and sink, rape and kill all those that I subdue.
Aboard 'The Phantom' pirate ship on our extended sailing trip
this brackish life is never glum, with stolen streams of potent rum
and stacks of stimulating snort
and willing whores in every port,
adventure cross the oceans with no boundaries to hold,
with tall tales that keep growing
and some as yet untold!

[Of sailing to edge of the world, steering along it's brim,
of being swallowed by a whale during my daily swim,
of climbing up it's blowhole to then surf upon its spurt,
till spinning dive back to the deck concluding death defying flirt.]

Of surging chase at pulsing pace, in tactical decreasing space,
then comes the final broadside and the disabled embrace.
A sudden swell flows overboard to gush and flush out hallowed hoard,
face to face
hand to hand,
toe to toe contact,
savage brutal butchery has the desired impact.
The skull and bones are hoisted, another cross is bared,
now it's down to business, there is booty to be shared.
The Captain,
upon disclosure s'always subject to the yank,
the profitless are promptly prodded off awaiting plank.
They'll join the dead and decaying who bloat beneath the waves,
the women will be servile. Until sold on as slaves.

Of natural islands, native charms,
beaches fanned by swaying palms,
of disfigured immoral knaves, convoluted cryptic caves,
selected moles, excited holes,
treasure maps and booby traps,

"avast lips from your utterings", but this I will disclose.

I've jewel inlaid regalia, with crowns destined for kings,
I've diamond, sapphire, emerald, opal, pearl and ruby rings.
My caves hold that much silver you'll be blinded by the gleam,
there's riches on this island way beyond your wildest dream
and though you do not know me, I need you to be bold,
for to me,
you are simply worth your wait in gold."

I hope my friend,
that you don't mind my presumptuous pirate presence,
but I'm presently encountering a prolonged state of impotence.
My ignorance of bearings was the way our problems started
as we entered seas more bountiful, but as of yet uncharted.
Sighted by flotilla, headed by the Kings own ship,
we took evasive action so as to give them the slip.
Manoeuvring for days, engaged upon an unknown course,
bellowing instructions till me vocals had gone hoarse.
We finally reached
out of sight, then set about to find,
a place where we could leave all of our current foes behind.

Arising on horizon, a haven came to view,
appearance? uninviting, but for just now it would do!
Encircling we scoured looking out for suitable docks,
that's when we smashed into the jagged barnacle encrusted rocks
which lay beneath the lapping tides, their aim was just to wait,
immersed until the time that they could seal a pirates fate.

While 'The Phantom' broke up slowly, everyman aboard,
was quite able to save himself whilst rescuing my hoard.

This island,
remote and foreboding, has definitely not
up until now, been a place where an **X** marks the spot.
Those who came ashore did quickly dwindle to a few,
then finally I dispatched the last member of my crew,
blighted by their knowledge, they died from what they knew.

Now solitude has taken hold,
I'm tired of counting gems and gold.
I have a whim, now here's the thing,
I fancy one last filching fling
and if you follow carefully the flow of these contours,
half this awaiting treasure, will instantly be yours.

But hurry now I beg you, for time is getting short,
I long for re-acquaintance with those characters from every port
and so I pray these words I write will not decay to mottle,
before you get the chance to read, this message
in it's bottle.

Oppressed

Oh ye of cold, deceiving tongue,
purloiner of my peoples pride,
you crushed the fabric of our world
until we lived
as you decreed.

Scattered, blown to barren lands,
battered by your winds of change,
incarcerated and condemned for crimes of inconvenience.

As arrows,
hearts were broken,
desire emerged in ghostly dance,
to resurrect the life we'd known,
restore our tribal legacies.
Still, fork tongue
did not leave us,
desolation took its toll,
inflicted wounds became too deep,
scars that time can never heal,
but though repressed, *"we shall not yield!"*

Those winds of change will fan the flames that flicker hope within.
Desire for reparation,
will burn through age from loin to seed.
A simmering intensity
that can only ever be
doused by native liberty and freedom of the plains.

The elders have been summoned and the wisdom they bestow.

Cast aside historic chains,
grasp and steer the guiding reins,
then venture out on to the plains and ride,
ride,
not from the trespassing foe,
but once more with
the buffalo.

What was that?

Lurking amongst forestation, seeking unsuspecting prey,
the newly born or ageing carcass, waiting for the lone to stray.
As if one with its surroundings, cloaked against the naked eye,
calling upon heightened sense, it has a lust to satisfy.

Engrossed amid the chore of eating, alerted by snap of branch,
bulging eyes, strain for movement, body springs to stricken stance.
Pulsing veins steer pounding blood, fear of the unsighted foe,
senses merge to form confusion, should they stay or should they go?
Twitching leaves add to the tension, still there is no earthly sight,
deciding to refrain from chance, the stiffened beast now takes to flight.

Prancing round rooted obstructions, dodging timbers rigid stance,
leaping brooks and dirty dimples, eyes are glazed in pursued trance.
Exertions drain innate resources, with each stride the hunters nearing,
streaks of light, soft rays of hope, then place the presence of a clearing.
Bursting into brilliance, an evasive weaving stride,
glances reveal naught behind, relief and fear collide.
Fleeing flames lick at lungs, fanned by rampant breath,
ensuing pain then slowly wanes, a small price for avoiding death.

Having managed to survive, averted natures selective weeding,
calmness overcomes the fear, thoughts return to frantic feeding.
All's as if it never happened, perhaps it never did!
perhaps senses had conspired to, construct a beast that lay amid,
the fears and frailties of a mind, consumed by daily trials of life,
existence plagued by constant threat, where ritual of death is rife.

These thoughts achieved a moment's lapse it little could afford,
for even that which is not real, should never be ignored.
A swish of grass, a spreading paw, the merest semblance of a scent,
what was coiled, now springs to life, instant impact, imminent.
Why it was, and how it is, that first lunge missed, we'll never know,
luck and instinct did converge to launch beyond the lethal blow,
but, the next incisive glance, sends the afflicted body reeling,
grasping jaws around its throat, begin to drain all sense of feeling.
Tightened teeth, clamped beneath, will leave their telling mark,
the light of day, turned to grey, then everything went dark.

Nurtured with neglect

Pursuance of elusive dollar, doting on each dime,
meant even from the earliest days, they could not spare the time.
Never enough ours in the working irksome day,
parenting was procedure, there was no place for play.
The disregard continued through the forming childhood years,
for those that are oblivious, they know not where it disappears,
momentous moments evolved, but the image went unseen
and so the age of innocence did swiftly turn to teen.

Emerging awareness raised, abundant bonding fears,
but awkward questions were dispelled, then fell upon deaf ears.
Made to feel an oddity, abandoned to conform,
a life deprived of attention was portrayed as the norm.
Rebelling hormones surfaced, reactions became terse,
what had gone before, now only served to make it worse.
Festering emotions cracked, deep fissures forced divide,
intrinsic bridges crumbled and the gap was left to open wide.

Adulthood and matrimony brought forth welcomed child,
a new beginning brought hope that detachment could be reconciled,
but broken, bogus promises and questions as to haste,
re-aroused the anger, resurrected the distaste.
For through a generation and although now reaching prime,
their priorities took precedent and still they could not spare the time.

Varied approaches yielded no reciprocating deeds,
selfish traits had detached them from thought of others needs.
Longevity is limited and they soon became old,
attempted warmth allowed to dwindle, died out in the bitter cold.

Tomorrow's promise now becomes the hardest part to bare,
for now that they are both deceased
there is no time to spare.

For the chop

"Well hello there Mr Reaper, you're looking rather grim",
the visitor chose ignorance
as I spoke to him.
Draped in robes of ebony and unusually blithe,
he slowly stroked a stone across his erect curving scythe,
then sliding fingers long its blade, he seemed satisfied
that striations incised in his bone would suffice as a guide.

"Just exactly what is it that I can do for you?",
I knew as they were spoken they were words that I would rue.

Lifting up his hooded head, the intent in his eyes,
made me, at first oblivious, begin to realise
that upon listed appointments he was scheduled to see,
by process of deduction in all probability,
the next name on his despatch list was more than likely me!

What conspiracy had twisted fate? I really did not know,
but regardless of the motive, I was not ready to go.
So as he manifested to his full and daunting height,
I quickly whipped out Tony, my industrious termite.
Now when it comes to timber he is certainly no snail,
chewing like the clappers he made short work of the stale
and as the lethal implement cascaded from his grasp
I grabbed and swiftly blunted it assisted by a rasp.
"A funny tool to carry round" is something you might say,
but I was taught being prepared would always save the day.

Appearing no less sinister despite losing his crook,
I reached to inside pocket and produced a comical book.
Flicking through the pages I arrived at thirty eight
and delivered lines of pertinence, before it was too late.

Menacing in stride he stopped to muse at what I'd said,
the corners of his mouth began to rise as they drifted into
the semblance of a beguiled smile that soon became a grin,
which manifested, with his mirth, till he was soon laughing.
Now that he had started, he knew not how to stop
as on previous assignments all he'd ever done was chop.
On it escalated till he rolled upon the ground,
the joke that I had told him, had obviously found
the dormant sense of humour that for so long lay concealed,
which now emerged to flourish from behind his sullen shield.

As he rolled, I walked away and hoped he would remain,
immersed in jubilation, so
he'd never reap again.

Geriatric Vigilantes

Old. Decrepit. Out of date.
Father Time is running late
and soon will come that final day
when mortal life will pass away.
But don't be fooled by what you see
as things aren't all they seem to be,
for ageing folk have had enough,
of all that 'GERIATRIC' stuff.

Years of elderly neglect
have paved the way for disrespect,
shameful taunts to failing ears
and total disregard for peers
till darkness brings confinement home,
relinquished liberty to roam
for fear of suffering attack
from reprobates who seem to lack
in any sense of moral worth,
a trait allowed to stem from birth.

Well from today they'll take no more,
it's time to even up the score,
they want it how it used to be
when valued in society,
but insolence will cease to alter,
till they force the fiends to falter.

So.
Cloaked in martial secrecy,
they've been training busily,
dedicated preparation,
as they seek some reparation, by
teaching those that think they're able to prey upon the weak and feeble
that as from now it all will stop,
with a Kung Fu kick and Karate chop.
Ninja Nannies spreading dread
with tightened band round wrinkled head,
and Grandads pugilistic zips
with newly inset plastic hips
[he'll jink and jab, ruffle, scuffle
sock your chops, muffle, shuffle].
Even those with walking sticks
can distribute some vengeful licks
and those immobile can still fling
any object they can swing.
They will not stop, they have no fear
persisting till the streets are clear
and only when that day has come
when all the hordes of ageist scum,
are brought to book and made to rue,
the day they beat us black and blue.

When elderly assaults all cease,
they will finally rest in peace.

Deserted and duped

Though crescent moon slits sable sky to penetrate the night,
conspiring clouds converge, succeed, in impeding it's light.
Desiccated, desolate, deserted by the sun,
deceiving dunes, indistinct, now drift to become one.

A simple simoom softly stirs the sand that chose deceit,
it shifts and sifts to gently cool the yielding grains of heat.
Secreted, inconspicuous, a patient readiness,
allowed the application of its conceding caress.

[Unproductive scything thresh and furious flailing
as grabbed and grappled ankles sank amidst consume and cling,
was futile, as was beckoning to absent unknown ears,
forlorn brings the dawning of my deepest, darkest fears.
For desperation's fight for life has constricted my breath,
progressive is the lonely slide to suffocating death.]

The strain is almost too much for my tilted, silted chin,
reluctantly it rests upon the quagmire that I'm in.
But hope remains within my grasp from drifters duped before,
allied in grief, they lie beneath, to form a transitory floor,
a pinnacle that preserves present future from that passed,
though I know not how much longer
this tiptoeing can last.

At my rainbows end

I placed a prism on my neck,
at first it was a coloured spec
which dwindled in intensity the longer that I paused.
Coaxed into activity
by decreasing longevity,
I found my bleak surroundings and the lifestyle were the cause.

In need of change from fashioned clone,
initial steps to the unknown,
were nowhere near as daunting,
as I,
at first,
had thought.
The spec grew to a looping arch,
a guide for liberating march,
though was this walk a whim or would it be what I had sought?

A distant glimmer caught my eye
as downpour drizzled, then was dry,
through fading colours I could see
that hope had not forsaken me.
For as I came to journeys end the rainbow cleared,
as did the strife,
beneath I found no pot of gold,
just quality of life.

Alone

I am so alone,
cus they are all the same,
teasing latent confidants whose motives are but lame.
Probers of defences taut and rigid from the flak,
a fortified resistance built by years of unprovoked attack.

They executed empathy, whilst revelling in intimacies,
exploring those weaknesses that had long lay suppressed.
Beneath the facade of support, obsessively they did extort
through layers of sensitivity that had long lay caressed.
Their final act of treachery was enacted by wicked deed,
regurgitating revelations for the scavengers to feed,
merciless they bore down to inflict their spiteful wrath,
cackling their prattle, oblivious to aftermath.
But from the blunt bombardment, came creation of a sure,
I became an island that no other shall explore.

And I am all alone,
cus they are all the same.
I'm so painfully alone
and they are all to blame.

Homeward Bound

The ruddy rain poured.
Falling it cascaded down,
impacting on the reddened ground,
coating all that lay beneath with penetrating stain.
An ant, stood wisely, underneath
the protective curve of a hanging leaf
and mused during the cavalcade,
the route back to the hill he'd made.

One hour passed with heavy rain,
his patience then began to wane
and so he set off at a pace
encircling the confined space.
Seeking freedom he would nudge,
but all around had turned to sludge,
and so he stalled and stood once more,
to let the time pass as before.

Another hour came and went,
but constant rain would not relent,
so summoning determined grit,
he charged and made a run for it,
the boggy mud made going tough,
but ants are made of sterner stuff.
Dodging raindrops left and right,
his destination came in sight,
but,
distracted by surging glee,
there was a drop he didn't see
which landed with a mighty splash
to end the insect's daring dash.

His lifeless body slowly flowed into a hole deep underground
and finally it came to rest upon a small compacted mound.
Moments passed, a twitching limb
showed that there was still life in him.
The groggy ant now coloured red
regained some sense and scratched his head,
for how after his daily roam,
had he found his way back home?

The Madagascan Wuggleworm

The Madagascan Wuggleworm
ejects a streak of purple sperm
which rises up to pinpoint, then contorts accordingly.
Each seeking jerked gymnastic gene
evades attempts to contravene
by swerving round obstructions during the trajectory.

As desired destination's reached
unwitting barriers are breached, by frenzy
of persistence to determined wriggling prise.
Then penetrations bursting spree,
swims on to prolonged pedigree
arriving in their millions, they poke and fertilise.

But Worm is never satisfied!
with constant lust, he aims to guide
and invade any orifice that strays into his sight.
So deeds proceed through rampant day,
a swollen discharging display,
creating tapioca trails which lattice till the night.
For that is when the tide does turn
and sprayed array returns in womb,
but those amassings purpose is to seal the perpetrators doom,
as females forced to fructify, encircle, confine, strive
to harangue till exhaustion,
then they eat the squirming worm,
Alive!

Presumed

People piss me off,
the low life and the toff,
the condescending ignorant who knows no part of me.
For no matter how I try,
the crux they judge me by,
is always a reflection of that which they choose to see.

**Treat each day as if your last,
for one day t'will be so.**

Marriage

Is marriage an institution?
Or is it merely the vehicle to drive you to one!

Friendship

A friendship drifts upon life's waves,
tides of time bring ups and downs,
but its voyage will only last
if both take turns to steer its helm.

Stupid people of the world. Unite.
On some suitably distant planet.

Suburbia

"Ooh look out their at number five,
they've got a new car on the drive,
they must have picked it up today,"

"and lost a fortune on the way,"

"and take a look at twenty four,
they've had new windows and a door,"

"the one's they had were good as new,
but old windows will spoil the view,"

"over there at thirty three,
they're building a conservatory.
Royal in style, stained, embossed,"

"it makes no difference what the cost."

[Gazebo, decking, enormous shed,
they've got more flowers in their bed,
hanging baskets, potted plants,
bigger, better, more, enhanced.
The Jones' really are the core. Those beside them **should do more**!]

"Just look at how their grass has grown,
can't they pay to have it mown? and get someone to clean their bin",

"before they put their rubbish in!"

[Wash the car three times a week,
polish, buff it, make it squeak.]

"They need to be respectable
it's really not acceptable.
it took us time to get this far",

"oh will you stop your BLAH, BLAH, BLAH.
  It matters not if those nearby, conform to rules that you live by,
  return the curtain to its place,
  permit your neighbours minor grace."

[To those that have not yet succumbed,
or slowly had your spirit numbed,
don't strive to be another Jones,
Suburbia has enough clones.]

The Root of all Evil?

666
the number of the beast,
dining with the dozen as they eat the final feast,
infiltrating weaknesses
when you need him least
he'll be there.

Just as he is, when he was,
narrating with the Nazis as a solution was found,
stirring the tsunamis till all dissidents are drowned,
masturbating masses, so as swarm can become plague,
draining till dementia leaves a hollow carcass vague,
causing menstrual misery, firking in the womb,
dabbling with destiny, determining doom.
He permeates the patterns, nurturing sadistic urge,
he riddled rampant rodents so the buboes could emerge,
he compresses the global plates, grinding till they quake,
levering the avalanche, he coerces each flake.
He agitates the hatred amongst members of the Klan,
he paints conflicting colours on the canvasses of man,
he sows the seeds of anarchy, he instigates the brawl,
fury, madness, conflict, death, he thrives upon them all.
Twirling the tornadoes,
hurling hurricanes,
igniting the kindling, fanned infernal flames,
raging with intensity, burning in degrees,
the charred remain a testament to his atrocities.
To turn our world to shadow is his all consuming aim,
yes, for everything that's evil,
the Devil is to blame.

Or is he?

Hoggin the togs

A chill bites in the dead of night,
"again the duvet's taken flight",
as usual the thermal strands are in the clasp of pilfering hands.

I sit upright and feel for prize
success! achieved through bleary eyes.
A little tug, it will not budge,
persuading words, an urgent nudge,
but nothing stirs,
"I'm gunna freeze",
do I beg on bended knees?
Alright! the times come to employ,
a swift snatch, though it will annoy.
Slinking hands, reach out, take grip
the yank succeeds to give the slip,
"I've got it!",
"Oi, you've nicked the cover",
my smug retort
"go get another",
they grab it back, tis as before,
now bed becomes a tug-o-war
with pull and pull and pull till tear
has innards flying everywhere.
The light goes on, emotions stewing,
a few deep breaths,
what are we doing?

A long embrace, a peck, a kiss
intensifies till swollen bliss
delves to those depths that cease with hilt.
With heat like this,
who needs a quilt?

Taking it too far

"Hello,"
"Hello,"
"and how are you?"
"and how are you."
"I'm fine thankyou,"
"I'm fine thankyou."
"Well this is strange,"
"well this is strange."
"Your copying me!"
"your copying me"
"OK."
"OK."
"Thwabble babble,"
"thwabble babble."
"obble bobble,"
"obble bobble."
"peppermint worm,"
"peppermint worm."
"icy fire,"
"icy fire."
"have you got a name?"
"have you got a name."
"tell me is it Peter, or could it be Repeat?"
"tell me is it Peter, or could it be repeat".

"Well that was fun,"
"well that was fun."
"OK, no more,"
"OK, no more."
"look, you've had your joke, there's no need for a parrot anymore."
"look, you've had your joke, there's no need for a parrot anymore."
"I've no time for this!"
"I've no time for this."

"stop following me!"
"stop following me."
"do you mind?"
"do you mind."
"yes I do!"
"yes I do."
"will you leave me alone?"
"will you leave me alone."
"I need to go to the toilet!"
"I need to go to the toilet."
"take your foot off the door!"
"take your foot off the door."
"I'll call the Police!"
"I'll call the Police."
"now cut it out!"
"now cut it out."
"**I'm warning you**,"
"I'm warning you."
"**one more chance**,"
"one more chance."
"punch me hard,"
"punch me hard."
THWACK!@!*
Now who's a witty Polly!

The time of your life

Tick, tock, tick, tock, tick, tock, tick, tock,
tick, tock, tick, tock, tick, tock, tick, tock,
your time begins
tick, tock, tick, tock,
you emerge
tick, tock, tick,
immersed asperge
tick, tock, tick,
hormonal surge
tick, tock, tick, tock,
carnal urge
tick, tock, tick, tock,
marital merge
tick, tock, tick, tock,
impregnation, duplication, aspirational regurge.
Tick, tock, tick, tock,
tick, tock, tick, tock,
duty's doth diverge,
domestic or servile concierge.
Tick, tock, tick, tock, tick, tock, tick, tock,
tick, tock, tick, tock, tick, tock, tick, tock,
unending scourge
tick, tock, tick,
forties resurge
tick, tock, tick, tock,
freedoms purge
tick, tock, tick,
decay's converge
tick, tick, tick, tick,
on deaths verge
tick, tock. Tock.
Your time comes to its end. Loved ones do attend.
Lamenting now in harmony
with parading funeral dirge.

72

Unwanted delivery

Whimpering discontent,
fret amidst the woven weft,
clamber of the condemned
nuzzles crave immunity.
Rhythmic calculated march,
black, bereft of clemency,
cocooned inhumanity
through indolent decree.
As sought seclusion manifests,
confining clench slips into curve of retracting release,
tossed indifference,
executing deed,
harks frantic yelps from unweaned whelps till whimper is no more,
asphyxiations sound is drowned,
dragged down to the darkened depths,
abandoned to decay.

What is that I hear? Could it be your conscience calling?

As it stands,
we're in the hands
of subjugating global brands,
exploiting extractors of disposable currency.
Corrupting games
by woven names,
oblivious to whom it maims,
commercial commerce, immersed in coercing abject poverty.

So in your lust
to have a must,
whilst spending beyond hard earned crust,
intoxicated by the rush of fleeting happiness.
It could be thus,
you feel disgust
for those whose actions are unjust,
if so, break from conditioning
and help those who have less.

Ease my suffering

I'm lying in a pool of piss,
who would have thought it would come to this,
these limbs are limp, the bed is sore,
cancer has riddled to my core,
now morphine is the only cure, who'll take the pain away?

Consigned to failing memory has gone the vibrant life,
joyous, playful escapades with children and adoring wife.
That zest was infiltrated,
then came days of dismay,
debilitating disease struck, advanced, till it took her away,
but though we're separated, she's waiting patiently.
Once more comes the agony.

This pain is more than I can bare, it gnaws me from within,
flailing with the torture sends my senses to a spin.
[Assembled family are distraught]
but please don't be morose,
just think of rising pleasure
as you increase daily dose.

"Please!",
don't linger in confusion,
administer desired conclusion,
finish this decay.

Then a tender hand of mercy
reached
to help me on my way.

Retribution

"Remember me?
 Do I ring a bell? ",
just like the one that started hell,
the jingle jangle beckoned all,
a foot, a shove, accomplished sprawl.
"Still no idea ?,
 just think of school,
 I'm the one you'd ridicule,
 I'm the one you'd always seek,
 the one you'd always call a freak,
 the one you used to scare to death
 with vicious taunts from bawling breath".

[Daily I'd look through the glass
 to fear the end of every class
 As playtime loomed, where would you be?
 my head span with anxiety.
 Out through doors, onto alert,
 round nervous edges I would skirt
 or any action to avoid
 intimidation you employed. Like,
 flushing head down toilet bowl,
 all the money that you stole,
 kicking, punching, slimy spit,
 rubbing face in piles of shit,
 hateful hands round throttled neck
 degraded to a whimpering wreck.]

"Isn't it strange! how those defiled
 by nature are the meek and mild,
 easy targets for your scorn,
 wishing they had not been born.
 Big ears, goofy, ginger, fat,
 derided cus **YOU** were the twat,
 not fit to walk upon the earth,
 misunderstood?
 no, drowned at birth!

Well what's it like now sitting there
with limbs tied to my reaping chair?
This knife I hold is not for show,
it has a purpose to bestow.
Go ahead!
plead and shout,
no one can hear,
there's no way out,
there's no way now you can avoid
the tit for tat to be employed.
Yes I,
like you,
will inflict pain,
but you will never hurt again".

Chocolate and Cheese

I killed a mouse today!

It had the nerve to notice and then nibble at my stems,
nurtured seeds of carotene,
blooming, green and succulent until gobbled away.
All I saw was red.
Now I want it dead.

On the very next evening, I watched to gauge its route,
curious, but cautiously it trod upon its garden path,
till nibble, nibble, nibble, munch, the anger swelled inside,
eating at my pride,
I'll have its tail upon a nail
I will not be denied.
Tomorrow I shall scupper.
This feast was its last supper.

I stewed throughout the day as I mulled mouse audacity,
feasting on my laboured love, what damned effrontery.
How dare he come onto my plot,
these lush legumes are all I've got,
their stems weren't coaxed to be defiled
by vermin's venture from the wild.

So with the night about to fall, I crouched down, hidden and astute,
I waited for appearance and then set off in pursuit.
Scamper, stop, scamper, stop,
by God! this mouse is quick,
not once have I come close to hit with my avenging stick.
Thrusting stab, lightning strike, no matter what I try,
a glint of mocking impudence remains upon its eye,
and that's when its not vanishing without a single trace,
only then to re-appear in unrelated place.
This is no good, I can't keep up, this chase will have to stop.
I'm out of breath, I must retire, before I simply drop.

Sinking into leather,
pondering endeavour,
fuming from the failure of my frantic escapades.
Needing a solution
to allow retribution,
I sit seeking a remedy to robbing rodent raids.
Let me see.
Poison? pellet? pouncing cat? a mouse trap would be swift,
a single sweet decisive snap to end this ravaging rift.
Mind over splatter!
Yes!

At the local hardware store, dwindling facility,
a craggy, bearded, short old man, stands to attention eagerly,

"I need to catch a little rat to end a prolonged spree",

"well sir , we have stacks of stock, the price is low, the advice free,
normal, flavoured, sensitive. Which one will it be?"

"I've come here for a mousetrap mate! not a pack of three",

"No sir, that's the settings and they're odoured to appease"
he leaned over the counter, his closeness caused unease,
then whispering his wisdom with a breath rank with disease,
"for guaranteed results I suggest chocolate and cheese."

A strange amalgamation was the first thought to my mind,
my choice had not extended past a meagre scrap of rind,
but who was I to question knowledge given by ironmonger sage
a glimpse of revelations generated through an age.
A look of pride and firm handshake accompanied the sale,
I left exchanging pleasantries, convinced my purchase would not fail.

A chunk made from the cacao tree and cheddar from the fridge,
were ground with haste into a paste [to gluttons, sacrilege].
Right then.
Place the bait. Tension bar. Set release [then] **THWACK**

"BASTARD, BASTARD, BOLLOCK BALLS"
the shock takes me aback,
shaking off contraption, after glance for severance,
there follows a unique, unrehearsed, all consuming prance.
"Water, water!" dash to sink. Cooling, soothing flow,
pulsing tips, slowly restore, from the sudden blow.
Doggedness now intervenes to urge me through persistent snaps,
the practise in precision soon results in prolonged snapping gaps
till stubbornness pays off and with the tension set to slight.
Carefully positioned.
It now awaits the night!

Tick, tock, tick, tock, tick, tock, tick, tock,
tick, tock, tick, tock, tick, tock, tick, tock
I've lost count of how many times
this clock has sounded antique chimes,
but what I know is each strike becomes louder than before.
More beads perspire from anxious pores
the longer that the mouse ignores,
has roving enemy lost its inclination to explore?
Back and forth, too and fro, a pacing, chasing, plagued yo-yo.
But every time I go to see,
the empty trap waits patiently.

Evening came and went, then heavy lids fell with the night,
drifting to abyss, then
[STARTLE] afflicts renewed sight,
"what was that?"
the torch is grabbed, could there have been mishap?
frantic steps rush to location,
light reveals an untouched trap.
"Oooh this damned confounded mouse is drivING ME **INSANE**"
what wrong has been committed to be cursed with such incessant bane?

My seeping, swollen, reddened eyes, blur me into bed,
through exploits I'm exhausted and my body lies jaded.

The chorus of the early birds alerts me to the morn.
Unaccustomed eye's slowly regain their sense of sight,
whilst palette craves the taste of brew
till rising rituals fulfilled
and boiling bags are gently stirred, gently poured, slowly sipped,
"aah, that's so much better. But wait!
where is the trap?
has there been a theft?
it's not where it was left!
has the tyrant taken it?
I fumble awkward keys,
at last the lock agrees
to allow access to the rear,
where chill of morn has no effect upon my intrigued frame,
but where's the culprit that's to blame?

Upon closer inspection,
I sense merest reflection
upon a cracked distorted pane which allows me to see.
That huddled in a pot,
having succumbed to my plot
was the mouse who'd dragged the block in fretful attempt to be free.
I turned the crock triumphantly.

There it was,
trapped by Legge,
though paralysed, it was not dead,
the impudence in stride had now been
reduced down to dread.
"take a nibble now!", mocked I,
"suddenly you're not so sly".
But stiff, it just looked up at me,
seeking human charity,
sensing none it made a final vain attempt to flee,
unsuccessfully.

It's rampant cage, ravaged by breath,
increased in rate, foreseeing death,
care?
not I!

too busy was the sift through yonder pile.
A block of wood to make it quick,
this was no job for flimsy stick.
Raising fatal log the fear emerged to grip its transfixed eye,
but vengeance knows no clemency, its time had come to die.
It scuttled to deceive oaks kiss,
but I made sure smash didn't miss,
then subtle crack of breaking bone arose from that beneath.

The stake was raised, expecting death,
I was surprised, it still drew breath,
a twitching body's crushing strife,
embroiled in fight for right to life,
then spasm struck
and bubbled blood did surface from it's core,
gasps for air diminished till the creature's struggle was no more.
Life just drained away,
twinkle dulled to misty grey.

Immersed in outright victory,
a sudden surge washed over me,
euphoria subsided as I glanced down to the ground.
Through rampant egotistic craze,
perception emerged from the haze,
as feeble carcass, stricken stains, squashed remains
lie, limp, lifeless, distorted, but their impact is profound.
What was it that possessed me till wicked deed was done?
the jubilation turns to shame of turning slaughter into fun.
Remorse riddles, emotion swells until its volume falls,
absorbent sleeves tend to the needs of blubbering eyeballs.
I slowly lift the trap,
the muted mangle swings beneath,
its pitiful appearance is the cause, which leads me to bequeath
that from this very moment to the day of my demise,
no other creature shall be killed, no matter in what guise.

The kitchen sink and drainer form a makeshift mortuary,
a service is conducted to atone for my debauchery.
Patterned towel wraps into shroud, a baked bean tin, becomes coffin,
lifted, mouse is processed to penultimate resting place,

awaiting wheelie bin.
Some words would be appropriate, an act in final bid,
to reconcile the wrong I've done, before I close the lid.

.... !
An open mouth though willing, has no notion what to say,
though thoughts manage to manifest despite prolonged dismay.
"I am so sorry Mr Mouse,
 forgive me, and my murdering way".

Warm Undercurrent

Betty Bladders incontinence
was perceived as a pestilence
by all of those that came within the near vicinity.
Comments and talk were always snide,
but no matter how she tried
she could not stop the dribble or the pungent smell of wee.
Acidic stains soon took their toll and urged her to go out and stroll
to follow taunting tongues, whose lash, had caused such misery.
You may well think her actions cruel
but when they visited the pool,
she'd swim in front
allowing
inhibitions to run free.
Gulp!

...................Of a son

I see the trauma in his eyes,
one day he'll come to realise
my words are for his benefit and not for detriment.
This onus upon every deed
is inspiration to exceed.

That spectre of expectancy allowed me no relent.
Domestic barrage drove a wedge,
incessancy pushed to the edge
until such time as his will could no longer bare to stay.
Love consumed to taint the boy
and ultimately did destroy
the bond I'd sought, has only served
to drive the man away.

Today

Today will burst beginnings.
Today will consume end.
Today will incur fracture.
Today can embrace mend.
Today could be momentous doing actions that inspire,
today could culminate in gaining that which you desire.
Today contains the unknown,
today is unexplored,
today is here for living,
there's no time to be bored.
That that's gone before you,
leave it in the past,
as for some,
this day could be your first,
or it could be your last.

Relative rebuke

Your father's, brother's, sister's, uncle's great niece
called today,
her auntie's, nephew's, brother's wife, told her to
"go away".
The husband's, sister's mum implored a better attitude,
her mother's, husband's, granddaughter said
she was "far too rude".
Her niece's, cousin's, uncle's wife then asked for a reprieve,
but with that kind of welcoming I said
"I'd rather leave".

Reformed Character

"Ship the bleedin bastards back to where they all belong",
"nigger, sambo, paki, coon" was spat with vicious venom,
a response generated by perceived invaded shores,
"keep your thievin hands off, wog, this land is mine, it isn't yours".
The rampant hatred festered in his narrow minded head,
enforced exile evolved into talk of wishing them all dead,
even the merest mention would result in racist rage,
a rhetorical reaction that epitomised the age.

So life progressed,
as it does
and incensed time began to tell,
years of damned intolerance conspired to make his health unwell.

Tubes down offending orifice, confirmed an ailing heart,
a delay would prove fatal, he would need an identical counterpart,
so placed upon a waiting list whilst the donor was sought,
he yearned for the replacement so his life would not be short.

The old rotating calendar, seemed slower than before,
frequent rest from labouring chest were ailments he could not ignore,
with days and nights decreasing and with faint and faltering breath,
the blustering orator
consigned himself to death.

It was as if by miracle a heart was found that matched,
prepared plans were enacted,
the eminent organ was despatched.

Pacing. Pulsating. Embracing. Placating.
Anxious hours stagnating amidst sustained distress.
Alluring doors, processional floors, plight implores, obscuring gauze
merge with jubilation's surge as surgeon speaks of the success.

Phased recuperation,
rising rejuvenation,
turned to contemplation as to he who'd sacrificed.
Probing investigation,
revealed origination,
overwhelming consternation struck........?
on finding to whom he'd been spliced.

Above details presented was the photo of a man,
ebony in texture, a distinctive African.
They looked upon each other with uncertain searching eyes,
as initial confusion lapsed,
they both came to realise.

The features placed before them was an image in itself,
peel away the carcass and you'll find reflections of yourself,
those qualities possessed, are generated from within,
they depend upon the person, not the pigment of his skin.

Humbled by experience, benevolence ensues,
his understanding, tolerance, love and respect accrues
and now that he has found the traits that once his soul did lack,
enlightenment has decreed that his heart's no longer black.

The price that you might pay

Immersed within a smouldering kiss,
stimulating sensual bliss,
actions primitively pure
succumb to attractions lure.

As urges to explore abound,
garments are thrown to the ground
till finally the skimpies slide
past pubic parts they scarcely hide.

Naked. Inhibitions bare,
caressing hands are everywhere,
tongue and teeth, lips and necks,
flicks and licks, nips and pecks,
fingertips then probe and tease,
willing eagerness to please.
Organs, swollen and erect
have no compulsion to protect,
desire to copulate grows stronger,
they try, but can't wait any longer.
Penetration. Long and deep,
lubricating fluids seep,
coupled, overcome by lust,
moaning to the rhythmic thrust,
escalating ecstasy,
intensifies till finally, release,
a swift and hard climax,
rigid, relax, rigid, relax,
then wilting from the rampant pace,
they partake of a brief embrace.

"You looked and I could not resist,
 my surging yearning to be kissed".

"As soon as you had looked at me,
 I felt an instant chemistry".

"That really was the hottest sex
and if it is you don't object
I'd love to do it all again,
until this lust begins to wane".

"Yes, I simply can't resist,
this inclination to persist
and now we're talking openly,
it's only fare that I decree
I'm positively H.I.V."

Epic

In the City of York, in the year of our Lord, 1776,
a renowned man is hassled, provoked, pushed till he afflicts.
This here is the story of the journey from his sins,
on cobbled stones of crimson, is where this tale begins.

A physique, forged by furnace,
a force, that couldn't care less,
a fiery unrelenting will no other man shall tame.
A parched thirst, quenched by tipple,
a willingness to cripple
and vicious temper merged into a knuckled night of shame.

Narrow remote streets ushered the encircling goading crowd,
animated gestures flailed, allegiances were aired aloud,
two agitated shadows scrapped by flickered tallow light,
but swagger swiftly turned into a damned uneven fight.

Pummelled to the putrid gutter,
pleading lips then ceased to utter,
features swollen from the frenzy twitched,
then death did lay immersed.
All then stood as stiff as bristle,
as they heard enforcement's whistle,
then in a flash, the scuttling voyeuristic rats dispersed.

But this current misdemeanour meant that with his long standing,
the provocation would mean nought and he would surely swing,
so the perpetrator Drinkette scorned and then took to his toes,
embarking on a routine route to evade his pursuing foes.
Down Slag Street, Piss Pass, Rancid Row,
the cutest course whilst lying low,
stopping systematically to listen acutely.
Fear now forced him to vacate,
so slinking through the Micklegate,
he slipped into receptive night and blended instantly.

Destinations dissipated for the destitute.
London lingered briefly, but they new of his repute.
Long curving Scar, awaiting Ouse did offer rippled lull,
on up through hedge and headstones,
before him lay the road to Hull.

Nicking a neglected horse,
spurred onto a cantering course,
the highway would be utilised as circumstance befits.
Ale from isolated Inns,
ill gotten gains to pay for sins,
the resources he'd left behind would be replaced by wits.

Through Dunnington, to Kexby, naked flesh at Wilberfoss,
at Burnby, the Kings venison accompanied a bracken'd doss,
whilst Goodmanhams persistent drams was more of what he sought,
teal at Weel, fawn at Wawn, swigging wine at Swine, then on to
piscine port.

The harboured anonymity,
beside the brawn and briny sea,
was perfect in its substance for absorbing drunken rogues.
Pilfering throughout the day,
evenings of disarray,
fascinating characters, spouting beguiling brogues.

"On one such ebony outing, I chanced upon a doll,
a most appealing buxom wench whose name was Jersey Moll.
Engaging me in revelry, we pranced the table tops,
her teasing tongue did tantalise between the flowing hops.
She introduced attentive friends, Just Jim and Honest John,
we swaggered te the shanties
and roared te vulgar rampant songs".
Coerced out over cobbles there then came a tacking whack,
the lively lights span furiously before the bracing night pitched
black.

"Woo hoo what a shindig, twas a night I shan't forget,
thy eyelids are cemented and the earth has not stopped swaying yet.
Whatever they were serving me it reached the required spot,
I remember only snippets, the rest is but a blurry blot,
for possessed smith could not surpass the pounding of thy head,
breathing feels so laboured, as if thy chest be dressed in lead
and though nought's passed these arid lips
there are persistent groans
and listing lubricated limbs
have failed te silence creaking bones
and can it be thy fuddled ears hear ripple of a stream?
do I lie by Kingston's swell or is this a concocted dream?
if so, twoud solve the sound of gulls in full and flowing flight,"
then sudden gasp and grasp for lost land
spurs conscious to present plight.
Instantly bolt upright to survey the bleary scene,
those that lay above him, and those he lay between,
were flung, as were the rodents to a renewed resting place,
the cloudy cleared to reveal that he would rather efface.
Defecated dripping stench, gripped by musty mould,
the dank dispiriting welcome of a ships confining hold.
His surging rage erupted as he stood upon the heaving floor,
hurling that which came to hand
he cursed as none had cursed before,

"damn those damned deceivers at the Crab and Cockle Inn,
a plague upon their accomplice", the inconspicuous Mickey Finn.
"Damn this ship and all aboard, curse their faring fate,
fetch the captain, bring him here, I'll tell him where te navigate."

Up above through grating, the numbers did accrue,
mocking insults flowed down from the resident seasoned crew,
whilst some of those shanghaied nearby whose mouths had become staid,
chose to voice opinions and did also join in the tirade.
[They did find that with me there will be no time to spout.
This fact became apparent as I swiftly knocked them out]

94

Then the ordered hordes descended
and at first were kept at bay,
it took ten men to harness me, though only one to flay.
For the verbal violent outburst, served only to consign
me to a fixed appointment with awaiting cat-o-nine.

A Marlinspike's silencing bite, did corrode thy defiant tongue,
the drummer boy began his beat,
the burly bosun's mate did mete,
as punishment began its vain attempt to right thy wrong.
Rhythmically the licking leather clawed at dogged flesh,
which soon began to falter from the unrelenting thresh.
The ruling lashes were repulsed until the tails did taint,
this day imparted wisdom,
I learnt the value of restraint.

Lifted to the bloodstained table,
'Doctor' did as he was able,
seeping wounds were left to wallow in a sea of coating brine.
Placed below toward the stern,
several mates took it in turn,
each relaying what would happen if I did not tow the line.

[One such man was William Crow,
whose legs were full of worm,
they'd riddled writhing passageways
throughout the oak that once stood firm,
but 'stead of asking Chippie to create by way of whittle,
he said his stumps were attached to the teasing of their tickle.
Besides it would be wrong to end their friendship with the lice.
Old Crow he made me laugh,
though his stench needed a bath,
but he proved the worth of friend,
loyal and noble to his end,
which would come as this man paid for me
the ultimate sacrifice.

Nigh on three weeks on me belly and the slits had almost sealed,
the fester had been kept at bay,
"be cautious till completely healed",
but wined and dining idle hands are considered a shirk,
so fester remutated to resenting he who did not work,
"for not one man amongst the crew
whilst sailing to and from the shores,
has ever been allowed to abscond from the grip of chafing chores."

Summoned to the Captains quarters,
as we reached unsettled waters,
prim and proper's pomp did promptly stress the need for discipline.
His eloquent express,
vividly did stress,
that a keel hauling awaited any re-offending harlequin.

Simmering compliance yielded to the man that guides the helm,
as existence is swift for rebels in this isolated realm.
Longevity still favours others more than it does some,
the calculating bide their time, till opportunity does come.

Awoken and forlorn,
well before the crack of dawn,
ejecting whistles turfed the sods to work allotted watch.
The Bosun set his tasks
and I do just as he 'asks'!,
as the eight bells signify the start, creating the first notch.

Scrub the deck with bible blocks,
feed the fowl and flapping cocks,
patch and furl essential sails,
prepare for forthcoming gales,
paint and grease,
caulk and seal,
do whatever's required to allow these wounds to heal.

ding ding   ding ding   ding ding   ding ding

The drifting shift is over and I'm ready for some grog,
oozing sweat has drenched me but the booze is worth the slog.
The Pursers Mate, fills measly cup,
but rations not a droplet more,
I tremble from the thought that this is all I have in store.

Cold and lumpy ageing oats which cling to form the rigid gruel
are handed with the sea biscuits as hard as granite rock.
They crawl with weevils, larvae, shit, to make the mornings fuel,
the only taste of meat we'll get
until cook serves the salted stock.

"Defiance!", now I'm on my feet,
it's time to mingle, spiel the deals,
theft has consequence here, so I'll use the gold stashed in me heals
to aid compelling persuasion for items that I need.
These acts are through necessity, they do not stem from greed.
So.
Limp Lung in the pantry did provide a personal keg,
a pipe from Thomas Cracklestone, a Broseley made by Legge.
Samuel Bunce the sailmaker, did deftly stitch a canvas sack,
that Hog stuffed with receptive straw,
which moulded to thy latticed back.
A cut-throat razor was imparted during a close shave
and nimble knife, though misdirected,
arrived from a chancing knave.
Some baccy in embellished pouch
came courtesy of Daniel Cane,
reluctant oilskins slipped from he who was not seen again.

ding ding   ding ding   ding ding   ding ding

The drummer boy purrrrupapums fictitious beat to arms,
inactive lids are opened to reveal their concealed deadly charms.

97

"Insert cartridge", wad then ram, shot, then final wad is rammed,
distincts interweave as one, for those that dawdle
shall be damned,
prick and pierce with priming tube, commence the hauling run,
expose the mouth, wedge and handspike, satisfy impatient gun,
pour powder to awaiting pan, cease the flow, retire,
pull the lanyard, trigger flintlock, knap the spark that hastens
"fire".
Latent brooding bellies fleeting furnace is unleashed,
shattering scatter lacerates a trail to those bequeathed.
Recoil, sponge, extinguish embers,
ignore the splintered or the slain,
summon that strength from within and do it all again.

ding ding   ding ding   ding ding   ding ding

Mealtime!
The stinging, smoky, choking swirl, lingers, strays, to slowly fade,
consumed silhouettes emerge from toil of rehearsed enfilade.
Cooling iron is secured, fashioned planks are laid between,
plates and grog are distributed, boy arrives with soup tureen
and serves the swimming pebble peas,
then returns to the source,
to fetch the feast that masquerades as appetising course.
Salted beef or salted pork, tough enough to bend a fork,
huff, accompanies lush thoughts of roasting hogs in York.
They fall to pigs in pen below and savour salivating slit,
which spurts to drip of sizzling fat, crackling back, basting,
baking ribs and bone and bacon, liver, kidney, trotter, tongue,
haunch, ham, hock, chop.
rotating captivation,
succulent gyration,
turns to tantalise the taste with trickle of the spit.

Those that lack the mental strength now succumb to the
spewing spray,
but they who have no stomach,
shall be left to waste away.
Only the fittest shall survive the voyage
within this snoresome ship.
So I finish all me chores,
pays a visit to the stores,
hitch me hammock and attempt to take
permitted quarter kip.

Rocked by creaking lullaby
and rhythmic sleepy sway,
set adrift to reminisce I swiftly doze me cares away.
Diving beneath creamy froth to swig the soothing malt,
refreshing velvet washes down the residue from meaty salt.
Clashing tankards multiply,
till shapely wench does catch me eye,
she strolls across provocatively,
sits beside and strokes me thigh.

Lewdly I admire,
the curves beneath lurid attire,
the lusting lick of luscious lips which whisper I'm in luck.
Clasping hold of groping hand,
she leads up stairs, through door to stand,
then hitches up her flowing skirt and offers me a !

ding ding   ding ding   ding ding   ding ding

"A pox upon this ruddy tub,
curse that bastard bell,
a fester to the crotch of he who brings me back to brackish hell",

"Cummon Drinkette move your arse, get busy from that bed,
 get yourself tied to the bow and spruce our figurehead."

The powder monkey Billy at the tender age of twelve,
Fabien 'Fathom' Mendez, an expert of the precise delve.
Nick 'Nimbleknot' Culdecott of roping interlace,
Renaud 'Flapflesh' Gigarpont, the man with half a face.
Zachariah 'Hooky' Luft, with scythe's instead of severed arms,
Slavor 'Scratch' Camdowski, possessor of flea bitten charms.
Walter 'Stitch' O'Mally, swift repairer of the sails,
Tribulynus 'Tonic', concoctor for all that ails.
'Donkey jaw' Dulce Donahue with curved protruding chin,
Coocoonau, a native cloaked from top to toe in vivid skin.
Hamish 'Fiddle' Hogmanay, the maestro of melodic tunes
and ornamental carver 'Ives'
etching our seafaring lives,
notching out the tusk and horn,
hunted, murdered, hacked then torn,
enabling the 'scrimshaw' to create
desirable boons.

The new watch is assembled then dispersed to undertake,
as the water sliced afore us whirls to trail a never ending wake.
Readying, steadying, hypnotic rippled eddying,
roping around fluttering waste, thy knee slides, "here we go!"
A sudden yank from Nimbleknot, who reconfigures the pivot,
then tells me with a tightening tug,
"Erasmus, take it slow."

Thy journey long the bowsprit to the dangle in mid-air,
is not one of those periods that pass without a concerned care
as improvising harness jolts and swings erratically,
above the drowning troughs and peaks of this immuring sea.
Fear of a detaching fling,
necessitates a sculpted cling,
'The Lady Apolina' and I meet for the first time.
The bolstering embrace,
now brings us face to face
and we look upon each other
through the layers of weathered grime.

Affinity is instant, rigid posture now reclines
to prize exquisite features and precision of her refined lines.
A dusty rag is dipped to drip,
then promptly dipped and dipped again,
immersed intoxication........
forces me to refrain
from placing further taint upon her oft neglected form,
overwhelming is desire which compels me to transform.
Several soft, determined strokes
onto her face and curling wreath
revitalise her essence and the effeminate beauty underneath,
I drift within the haze of each fastidious wipe and burgeoning buff,
thy task becomes obsessive. For is thy tinkering scrub enough?
Thoughts falter, mull, to alter from the notion of a tarted tree,
this Lady is the radiance who looks to guide our destiny.
A sudden rotten rag splats flush,
the drench provokes a raging chide,
but when I see Crow's toothless grin, thy fury does subside,

"please pardon the intrusion te yur blossoming duet,
 but ye need te get a move on or yur arse ull soon be soaking wet."

Sure enough beneath me, whilst engaged in resurrecting purge,
compliant waves had swollen to become an undulating surge.
"Aloft and furl the mainsail", comes the order from the poop,
racing up the rigging, those commanded, crab, grab, wrap and scoop
and battle gainst the bracing breeze
which wails through sails till gusting wind
is such that gales ferocity,
is one that God could not rescind.
Brooding clouds, once wisps of grey,
converge and writhe to thunderous black,
their muffled rumbles multiply till blinding flash, then deafening crack,
cacophony which coerces to summon volume from the deep,
massive waves then rise as mountains,
smash, cascade and swiftly sweep
across to bruise and bundle all that's unsecured upon the deck,

"Oh Lord, have mercy on our souls,
 do not forsake us to a wreck."

But squalling wind intensifies till whistle taunts the savage howls,
crescendo'd gusts emaciate the fear impressed pon exposed jowls,
frantic fingers grasp, rasp, grab the tethered lines of life,
doubting demons emanate to feast upon dissenting strife.

"**HOLD FAST**", I say to one and all,
come brace yourselves for we must check
this reeling course that's been imposed,
come rally round, "**ALL HANDS ON DECK**",
"**REDUCE THE SAILS, REEF IN TOP COURSES**",
insert that which "**REINFORCE**"s,
"**RUN BEFORE**" this deadly wind,
"**STEER HER TRUE**", do not rescind
or allow either side to slump,
now clear the bilge lads, "**MAN THE PUMP**",
"**PRESENT HER SIDE**", to swollen sea
and pray that God bestows mercy,
for if we're struck, she will capsize,
to flounder, fill, disintegrate before our very eyes.
Prelude to demise.

Twas then residing daemons who'd been waiting patiently
rose up to clutch the exposed keel and cant us to catastrophe.
All aboard was flung toward the listing larboard side,
that which lacked in purchase hurtled overboard to fatal tide
whilst those behind were left immersed
in gripping battle to contrive
a means of weathering this storm and keep themselves alive.

Ever on, the crests coerced careening, steepening tilt,
until resistance teetered just below the bulwarks hilt.
Thy hold upon the capstan's bar was true,
but under stress it snapped,
the unexpected weakness gave me no time to adapt.

Frantic arms could not prevent the icy plunge as water waved,
submerged and drawn down to the depths,
I knew I'd not be saved.
But not for first or last time, thy judgment proved me wrong, for
there'd been a guardian angel watching over all along.
Will Crow, unbeknowns to I, had slid a hook around me belt,
in between the to's and fro's it was an act that was not felt
until the tug from he above who grappled with thy fate,
as 'useless' legs gave leverage
whilst wedged within the Fore Hatch grate.
[Years of shipshape shuffling had produced shoulders strong as steel
and with a winching clinch of iron, his wrists began to reel.]
Surfacing to flounder as a fish caught in a net,
spluttering, I reached, then rose
to see to whom I owed the debt.
"I should have known!"
of those aboard, that it could only be him,
for who better could assist a dear friend
caught out on a limb.
[The instant was but fleeting where relief and gratitude overlapped,
expressions needed no words,
but silence ceased
as main mast snapped]
Faithful fibres splintering fray
furthered desperate disarray
as staggered timber succumbed to allure of fractures fall.
had ship encroached upon a curse
which strove to make dilemma worse,
now Davy Jones's Locker seemed to beckon one and all.
This summoning turned imminent for recent saviour Crow,
for precautions he had taken
served to drag him neath the lapping flow
as rope that he had tied from 'secure' mast to round his waist,
did promptly follow detached pole,
to whip away with haste.
Plucked from practical strappings, two stumps were left behind.
Testaments of valour from the man who felt inclined.

Beseeching vowels and consonants were bellowed till me
words went hoarse,
they carried briefly, but soon drowned,
consumed by elemental force.
Thy fear of suffocation battled gainst will to amend,
stricken, I extended,
but I could not reach thy friend.
Desolation overwhelmed, truth abandoned hope.
Mood descended with thy gaze to rest upon..... attaching.....
rope?
thy ponder spun with weave of hemp, to last,
what seemed an age,
till grasp of its significance,
caused rise and stride toward vantage.
Tossed and turned and ridiculed by tempest's unleashed whim,
my tormentor had not foreseen the extent of thy inner vim
as clamber to the poop, lurching cling on to the mizzen mast
provided secure mooring, turning hook into a holdfast.

Hauling in tenaciously,
ripped blisters began burning,
but nought shall stem the endeavour created by thy yearning.
To and fro the struggle strained
and mortal strength already drained
began to falter as each breath became a heaving gasp.
It matters not, length of extend,
the rope, it seemed, possessed no end,
now spectre of submission strives to snatch it from thy clasp.
But the fiery flame of fortitude that blazes deep within,
shall not be snuffed by exploits performed on thy sodden skin.
The slapping waves washed over me
whilst stubbornness persisted,
then drawing on reserves that I'd, till now, not known existed,
I raged against the rage that had exerted to consume
for nought will now distract me from thy efforts to exhume.

"**THERE!**", there, a head, bedraggled features that I know,
the vision that I'd strained for, the carcass of old Crow.
Concerted heave swept him aboard,
though final tugs were as if lead,
but spattered splutter leaked that the 'Old Bugger' wasn't dead.
I dragged him close and hugged him
as I'd never hugged a man before
and as one we'll remain lashed
through this ships unending yaw.

SEA. Sea, sea, sea, sea, sea, sea, .sea, ..sea, ...sea, ...sea.
Sore,   sore,   sore.
SEA. Sea, sea, sea, sea, sea, sea, .sea, ..sea, ...sea, ...sea.
Sore,   sore,   sore.
Creaking's, salty, silted tilt does rise and fall with aimless drift,
a journey instigated by the spineless rudders flitting shift,
now eerie silence deafens amidst timbers weary fret.
This strange disabled discord
for surviving ears is dulcet.
Encrusted eyes, crack their seal to witness skies of vibrant blue
and cast their gaze upon the remnants of attempted slew.
Fatigued bodies, flaccid, benign writhes remain in check
whilst little else remains upon the decimated deck.
Tattered sails,
battered rails,
limp rigging wrenched out strand by strand.
Missing masts,
floating casks,
an open space where cursing cook and galley once did stand.

A solitary sunbeam radiates a penetrating glow,
it strikes the jaded shadow from the silhouette of sleeping Crow
to emanate and brighten crewmates in this moment we derive,
any kind of reason as to how we're still alive?

[From a crew of seventy two, we've been reduced to ten.
Stricken shells who braved the swells to become ghosts of men,
lost in their direction
now the hierarchy's gone,
who will guide the missing helm to toil in abandon?]

The first day became rummage of, to rescue what was found.
The second saw dispersal of the tainted and the drowned.
From third to tenth we took to bucket, pump and shifting weight
because this ship would not repulse more cruel waves
angled as she was.

On eleventh she was righted, celebrating camaraderie.
On twelfth we stored provisions and began to disagree.
Twas then, eye's of uncertainty began suspicions rove
for twas obvious with meagre left not all of us would throve.
With thirteenth came assessment of remaining destitutes,
which of them were useless
and which of them had attributes?

Thomas Cripp, the carpenter, will be of use upon this trip.
The blustering braggart, Black Eye, will not even get a sip.
Coocoonau could subsist in whichever place on earth,
William Crow's the only man that need not have a worth.
Grindle Grack, the Bosun's mate,
will get his meed for every lash,
Osiah Rimes will take his side when it comes to the clash.
Hogmanay, though he's done nought, I can not eat laments,
whilst Mole, the mute, will incur a more permanent silence.
Tonic will be needed for his medical mastery,
lastly, come now let me think, oh yes, of course, it's me!

The fourteenth lay indulgent banquet
on which fear for life could feast.
The fifteenth brought collusion as the whispers were unleashed.
On sixteenth, isolated huddles urged each to decide.
On seventeenth allegiance manifested to divide.
On eighteenth stealth sought out those items deemed worthy of theft.
The nineteenth, confrontation came
between those with and those bereft.

"Damn you Drinkette and yur band,
 skulduggery has stripped ship bare,
 yuv left us nought to eat or drink,
 now give us our fair share."

107

"Steady on there Bosun's gob
remember now ye have no mob
I'd be extremely careful as te what it was I said.
He who last accosted me did rant and now he's dead."

"Do not think that dread resides in those, gainst you, who lack,
this ship is a small island, so yud better watch yur back."

Drinkette's rage erupted with a calculated pace,
a glinting swipe arced purposely to almost slice his face.
The carve reversed, but missed again,
then smash fractured Grack's jaw,
his jolted body reeled to stumble backward to the floor.
Swiftly before blear could clear, the hand was grabbed,
it's elbow snapped, a piercing screech dilated as his wrists
were swiftly frapped
and wrapped then dragged until the hoist ascended to the
burnished spike,
dangled pause was fleeting,
then hardened rope, assisted strike.
Slapped and slapped and slapped till its connection became thud,
the rhythm turned to frenzy,
Grack's flesh spurted its blood.
[Squirming screams for mercy ricocheted from repulsed ears.
Whilst rigid feet stood passive, influenced by intervening fears]
Finally descending, whimper crumpled to a slump,
condemning knot was released, hastening the corpse's flump.
Drinkette scowled through glaring eyes to inspect those assembled,
as mists of madness cleared, but its intensity still trembled.
Not a single head could raise the courage from its bow,

"Take a look now one and all and hear thy solemn vow.
 Should it be in future that ye fail te condescend,
 I shall deal as I have dealt and this will be yer end."

Fumbling the deadweight, grip raised trophy to the sky,
then cast that passed down to the vast with vehement outcry.

On twentieth, compliance doffed, but its resentment festered.
Critical conscience niggled Crow, so subtly he pestered,

"Can ye find it in yer heart te include them in carve.
Twould be unjust te forsake and then let the outcasts starve."

"Where there once was sentiment, the type of which ye speak,
there came a hail of chiding spurns till final pierce from selfish streak
detached thy contemplation as te that required by others need,
it is by this conviction, thy endeavour doth proceed.
Now, can thee refrain from constant overprobing of thy ear,
be content with privilege and except what I've bought thee here."

Producing from behind him came, "the lengthenings ye lost,
I had Cripp make these fe thee," I awaited no riposte.

On twenty first came buffeting which distracted thy stance,
twas then that Black Eye deployed aim to seize his ultimate chance,
a shot from procured musket burst and anxious ball did clip me ear,
I raised a hand to touch the gush
then turned me scowl to face the fear
impressed pon perpetrator,
who fell to his knees resigned.
An act of desperation from the man that felt maligned.
I could not muster empathy, but thought his deed was bold
and so instead of drowning, I chucked him in the hold.
I could not spare him rum,
so filled two casks, one piss, one sea,
I lowered them, said "Take your pick, makes no diff'rence to me."

On twenty second, arid's thirst drove those that lacked to grab a keg,
the act was swiftly thwarted and the trio clasped their hands to beg

"Dear Drinkette, bestow mercy, don't desert us to the parch".

Dropping to their knees, they bent to form a craved triumphal arch.

Then Crow renewed his beseech and the mute began to wail,
the time had come for scruples to be scaled against me ale.
I faltered, vexed, to mull the chorus pleading for thy charity.
Begrudgingly I nodded,
"but him below still gets me pee."

The twenty third saw last of some foods,
whilst the rest has dwindled low,
this truth is not so daunting whilst we sup a steady flow.
The deprivations driven Mole
down to the depths on nightly prowls
to burrow mongst the nooks and niches,
ferreting rodents from the bowels.
Thy cunning calculations conclude
that their fresh stocks outweigh thine,
so for sake of 'all' aboard, I reinstate their rationed dine.
On twenty fourth, strange utterings arose from captives tomb.
Solitary dialogue, regressing to and from the womb,
expletive doused delirium, distorted blasphemous emit,
but remonstration only served to fuel rant from the culprit.
Ramble, ramble, on and on, till tone became abrasive drip,
which clawed at brittle senses until sanity began to slip.
So Fiddle without instrument, began to sing a soulful tune
which increased to a resonance that nullified the loon.
The tussle pitched till twenty sixth till hoarseness forced a silent score
and as the hush descended,
the ramble was no more.

On twenty seventh, meat has gone
and moss matures on unscrubbed decks,
and apathetic will endures, and Rimes has sprouted purple specks
which ooze to battered bruising, though I have not laid a finger.
Tonic pronounced scurvy, said we could not let it linger.
On twenty eighth the barren box has left a rigid biscuit each,
slowly they diminish as in turn I clasp, extend, to reach,
to offer this significance, perhaps the symbol of our end,
ritual, took for granted, the source on which our lives depend.

Coocoonau on twenty ninth, attached a rope, jumped overboard,
a deep sea dive to the unknown, conclusion?
unassured.
The displaced foam receded, several bubbles broke,
then there was nought
except the convoluted rope, which rippled dip till it was taut,
and so an eerie silence consumed those that salivated,
as they watched the line, their juices flowed
and hopes were captivated.

"E's been down there a fair long snort,
what is it do e think e's caught,"
impatient intrigue gripped Cripps thoughts of what he might receive.
The strain then twitched more than it ought,
it slumped te limp it thrashed till taut,
this cycle replicated, so I ordered the retrieve.
We grabbed and grappled to a man,
a shanty roused rhythmic elan,
excursion heaved the fibres, sudden slack backed us to floor.
Toppled to inelegant heap,
we floundered as if caught by neap,
then righting, we persisted as if hauling from the moor.
Tension resumed, attention wandered as to that attached to line,
was it dead weight of our native, or would it be serpentine?
Resistance rendered it alive, with two and froing friction,
would that surfacing be fabled, or would it prove fiction?
We did not have to wait long for our answer to emerge,
as rhetoric to rhythmic reel revealed with slashing surge
"a monster", white as Christmas snow,
with blades te sides and back,
it lashed until it reached thigh high, then launched into attack.
A thousand razors glinted from its gaping estuary,
we scattered to the nearest place which offered sanctuary,
we watched it writhe and wriggle as it
smashed against the empty kegs,
but though the beast be savage. It does not chase?
it has no legs!

Terror turned upon perception, those that froze proceeding flight,
thawed to slide from place of refuge,
courage stirred to confront might,
with rummaged club or cleaver raised to placate ravaged mood,
perceived peril had transformed into a feast of food.
Gingerly our stints were gauged twixt flipping flurry, gasping gulp
and on each time it paused for breath, we hacked its head to pulp.

["What was this sadist that we'd raised,
which grins throughout its lynch?
Whose detached eye, now looks at I,
though not once did or does it flinch."]

Ecstatic,
erratic hornpipes
jigged from stem to bow.
Then frolicking flow came to a staunch when,

"what about Coocoonau?"

All aboard stiffened to seize before they raced to starboard rail,
hurling hails and seeking strains, both came to no avail.
Furrow of the troughs and peaks has offered not a glimpse

"Seems sure e's etha bin consumed
 or become fodder for the shrimps!"

The mood of most assembled sank, as reminisce consumed,
had he succumbed to saturation, or would slit see him exhumed,
then from behind, utter surprise, when,

"What t luckin for?"

We spun to scarce believe our eyes which came upon a
sight for sore.

A dripping apparition, whose presence, plagued approach.
Warily, specific steps proceeded to encroach.
A single fingers quivering prod,

"he's solid as a post!",

bemusement sought,

"why due do dhat?",
"we thought ye wer a ghost!".
Revelry erupted to surround and hoist
he who exceeds,
celebrations acclaimed triumph of heroic deeds.
Twas then amidst festivity that Tonic touched the ooze of blood,
it flowed from missing little, ring and half of severed pud.

"PUT HIM DOWN, you lolloping clown, can you not see he's hurt.
As for the rest, hark my request to help me stem this spurt.
Stoke the fire,
then go acquire an iron, whilst I garrotte,
he'll need some froth and bubbling cloth, for bite, snatch him spigot.
Twill not be long now Coocoo,
so whilst we wait, why don't you spout,
recite all that there is to know on how this came about."

"Me dive, me lucky diddy fish, me see long way, me swim.
Me catch, me hooky diddy fish, me switch the rope, it skim.
Beaucoup fish bite, ya ya, two finger, diddy fish,
me thought me dead, beaucoup fish, swim way,
cum back, swish swish.
Me push rope in at beaucoup mouth, beaucoup fish ya ya,
rope swish gone, in hooky mouth, fingers, fish, go way, ha ha!"

" Seems to me, beneath the sea,
 a protector looks out for thee
 and guards against assailing foes
 to ensure though art blessed."

113

Then embered glow, brought spigots stow
and beads of sweat began to flow,
gripping, eyes blaze riveted, as molten sear is pressed.
Sizzle, fuelled the fumes of flesh, bloody boil encrusted,
stifle urged enamelled grate, twixt rage at he who thrusted.
Tugged and lugged the grapple wore till crimson seep had ceased,
limp and giddy from the gore, the native slumped, then was released.

On thirtieth, we sustained slicing slits and gluttonous gorge.
These tracts are acts which distract from 'The Lady's' inching forge.

"Huh, some lookout she turned out!
A pilot guiding from the maim!
more like it's she who should look out,
or chop might put her te the flame.

Thirty first, another day aboard this traipsing tub.
Rimes' teeth are falling out, despite the latest grub.
Cripp has chipped new rudder, it'll be long time afore it trails.
Tonic stays so selfless as he tends to all that ails.
Fiddles made, with aid of Cripp, a viol, from chestnut and gut,
with plaits of hair, racked for a bow, its strokes emit eerie gamut
which though they be unusual, soon soften, till they soothe to coax,
the wails and woes of burden, repressed through incessant soaks.
Its ribbed reverberations, have even penetrated Mole,
he stands and sways with rhythm,
tis as if the chords have touched his soul.
Coocoonau has fever, generated from his gash
and Crow's fell victim to the blight, in form of scurvied rash.
Tonic told us barrelled apples would be only cure,
so as the lubbers lay there heads, I sift secreted store.
A swig of potent cider, proceeds to tang and tickle lips,
then creeping out precisely, I provide Will with vital sips.

The thirty second? much the same. We're on to thirty third.
Despite the escalating lame, resolve remains inured.

There are some random rumblings which pang to perturbed spats,
it's no surprise now pantry's bare,
we've even eaten all the rats!
but fuddle to despondency, this dearth can be dismissed,
as long as there's provision for thy cares to proceed pissed.
On thirty fourth the hunger gnaws,
and shells have begun sprouting sores,
there is no bolster from the crutch as ale is down to dregs.
Delirium has taken Rimes,
to performed prancing pantomimes,
though acts cannot be recompensed, no matter how he begs.
On thirty fifth, his unpredictable madness was restrained.
On thirty sixth fixation stared and lifeless colour drained.

The torrid days to fortieth, bring boiling blisters, blight and banes.
Feebleness has fettered. Listless limbs. Still remains
are forced to face a future where the worst is now assumed,
this voyage upon unending seas is ultimately doomed.

[Why has land forsaken us? Why does it lay concealed?
Upon each new horizon, why won't a pinnacle rise congealed?
A fragment of solidity, the merest grain of hope,
a buttress to intoxicate, a tit to wean me from thy tope]

"Water, water, everywhere", but not a drop for Drink.
  Water, water, everywhere, bewitches to thy brink.

Forty first, raging thirst, rabble-rouse and rant,
surreal seduces its appeal to those forlorn and desiccant.
The writhing deck's reduced to speck, which
stretches to unending plank,
staid bones on board, now turn toward,
each roasting till a tasty shank,
thy ladle applies bastes with haste, as object becomes clearer,
thy ravenous race, increases pace, but advance is no nearer.
Vacant salivation deems to dribble with affectedness,
thy all, coerced by craving, craves coerce to coerce progress.

Thy desire attracts audience of elevated condensed crowds,
who snigger at predicament, then drift to masquerade as clouds.
Their spite invites inquisitive winds,
which probe, descend, deride with howls
to stir a hearty buffet
and distract thy grumbling bowels.
Intrigued rancid ripples rise to inflict mocking spray,
they aim to season juicy joints and savour thy dismay.
Reaching crusading cleaver, to sliver slice to foil their ploy,
thy raise is interrupted as a crow shouts,
 "Land Ahoy".

Do thy ears deceive me, does desire overwhelm?
Or does the tongue of madness lap to influence thy helm.
A shank. Cooked to perfection, sidles over, sprouts arms,
starts to shake,
a distant stimulation draws,
"I'm being shaken by a steak!"
whose marrow puckers garble till its letters link lines that I know,
then cavity mutates into imploring head of Crow,

"RASMUS, can ye hear me? can ye see me? can ye speak?

extending, pensive fingers reach, to give a confused cheek a tweak,
a pinch, a jolt, a joggle, any compress that illumes,
"we need no butcher here son."

Reality resumes.
The cleaver falls down to the floor,
"tell me, tis it true?"

a finger rose to divulge that which was long overdue.

"CRIPP, take Mole and free the fluke,
the rest, help cast the anchor.
LOOK LIVELY LADS, we need te graft
te seize that which we hanker.

Come my friends, summon strength and toil till lungs abandon breath.
Tis sure this tide will pass land by and take us to our certain death."

Resurrection faltered,
resolution overcame.
The tasks were undertaken.
Success roused feeble acclaim.
'The Lady' strained against restraint,
reluctantly she came to rest,
tamed by depths of gouging scrape and pummel of the crest.
But tether failed to tame her flee
and purchase slipped to set her free

"**LISTEN LADS**, we have one chance, we'll need to tow in tandem,
get chattels, seal them in a cask, make haste, but don't be random.
Watch yur weight, twill be the buoy pon which your life depends
we'll have to chance this current, though we know not where it sends.

[When all were done, a rope, a link of unity was threaded,
the gathered group gave each a nod, then descended to dreaded]

The water takes thy breath away, despite efforts of hampered sun,
splutter, splash, gulp and lash are bolstered with inspiring dun.

[Weary stroke by weary stroke the course before is cupped behind,
progressing ever nearer to our Eden in the sea.
Dreary stroke by dreary stroke
the ebbed encore is supped with grind,
our distress is no clearer and our speeds derisory]
"We're drifting with the dead wood!"

The teasing tows do tantalise.
Caught twixt ship and falsehood,
the lure allows no compromise.

Strength has dissipated.
Will has lost endure.
Resigned to what is fated.
Prayer enacts closure.

We coast contours of island, a tour lit by twilight.
Heavy eyelids rise to fall, fatigue concedes no respite.
Shrinking glimpses laze to last, image stirs contrite,
as intervening headlands pierce, juts 'Our Lady' from our sight.

~~~~~~~~~~~~~~~~

Senses slowly stir,
bottom lip has trailed to gape,
tongue tries coated slur,
discourse draws enamelled scrape.
Drivels dislocating etch,
topples tittles, closing speech,
cascade enforces wretch,
mucous merges surge to beach.
Spurted saline flushes remnants of residing grit,
postures churn relapses prone with settle of thy pit.
I darest not move or waken
lest thy faith be nought but dream,
for faith would lie forsaken, if all is not as it would seem.
[Better to engross thyself, indulge this bed which pads profile,
absorb the waves of toppled crests which trickle rippled cantabile,
cantata, stirring, rousing rustled chorus mongst the swaying palms,
fresh infused levanter, coating aromatic embalms.
Captivating, stimulating, too good to be true!]
But if this trance be sincere, then why does day star barbecue,
it burns thy nape and exposed limbs,
it brands thy crown to boil thy head,
it pierces through thy filtering folds, constricted pupils see but red.

So influence! Should stem from I, and soothing lotion will apply,
these beams shall be deflected by a gamp shading the sky.

Thy will is contemplated.
Thy angst shall alter aim.
Thy patience is frustrated.
Thy pelt remains aflame.

Squint, trembles to tearful blink, invading brightness blinds,
the sandman has worked overtime, his shovelled surplus, grinds.
Port eye's clog enforces close, alliance turns to shield,
remaining sight redresses hindrance, yielding reduced field.

A convoluting Crimble Crab, sidles, stops, prepares to grab
as elevated curious eyes, twitch, prospective feast.
Deciding that flotsam bears life and customary jetsam rife,
pincers retract, scamper goes in search
of that deceased.

"The Others!"

Recollection springs to kneel, to find all still attached,
they lie in lapped inelegant sprawls, as rope meanders slatched,
cept,

"no, **No**!"

say tis not true, say constrict has not noosed.
Stagger, drag, Crow's linkage binds, Crow's released, Mole's
throttles loosed,

"Oh dear god, what have ye done?
 what drove ye te take Mole?
 Had he not endured enough? Was his not an adequate soul?

Condemnation flowed from Crow as sinful strands were held in hand,
neglected contemplation's stow, bore misdirected reprimand,

"But"
"DON'T dare te deceive me, look there as his blue imbues,
  I'm tired of yur relentless quest te inflict cruel slews."

Then old man's deep despondent gaze was drawn to sight beyond.
Despair became uncertainty, his manner stemmed respond.
Following fascination, I came upon his view,
amidst lush bordering foliage there stood an askew queue.
Natives, naked cept for shells. Women, firm, ripe, nubile.
Muscular men, not threatening, instead each possessed
crescent smile.
They beckon with no weaponry, no malice seems to dwell,
they bear no such resemblance to fabled savage hell,
but vigilance?, harbinger, to that fact as yet unknown,
prevents the seeds of harmony from mingle and be sewn.
Still, there language without word entices faltering meet,
sensing sceptic barrier broke, they flow from trees to greet.
Slow but sure we are enclosed, by erect nipples, pimpled flesh,
tis though we're valued bove all else,
revered with welcoming enmesh,
which elevates us o'er crowd,
which swarms on jungles relished route,
we probe and pierce the leafy shrouds,
to clearing heaped with dripping fruit.
Cited on a focal point, bedecked with bangled florescent,
drizzled, rubbed in oiled anoint, we eat to guts content.

Later.
Length?
"I've no idea!", as belly convalesces bloat,
Fiddle, Tonic, Cripp appear with self same satiated gloat.
We slap and ramble disbelief at how our fortunes faired.
Inquirie's solace lingers brief, as death of Mole is aired.
Will reveals his feelings. A fleeting, scowling glance,
unjust fabrication wounds, till distract comes from carnal dance.

Wiggling, giggling, bouncing bounds. Conches, proud, erect.
Wriggling, jiggling pubic mounds, desire smites infect.
Cavorting, They're begging me! its handed on a plate!
Swift concern seeks present males,
what would they do to consummate's.
I eye them individually, but still their smile emits,
nigh, betrays a bracing bone, a threaded rib befits.
[I can't help but admire the rigorous efforts that they're making,
painstaking first impressions, they seem to give no thought of taking]

  Women.
"Oh the women!"

begin writhing to a lather,
revelation to behold, whores nearer, then they gather.
Engulfed, the dripping frenzy compels eager guests to stand,
snaking hands eel massage, salvation is at hand.
Led along to humid huts, the wanton hordes decry,
but do I have the energy?
Twould be rude not to try!
I'll lie back, think of England, be a distant diplomat.
Mounted, ridden, fervour hastens, gushing, 'evan'e'scent' scat,
"Arghhhhhhhhh".
Rigidity relinquishes,
She shagged so hard, I thought twould snap,
I'm ready to roll over.
Instead the idioms lick and lap
and cultivate another growth till straddle and consume,
rut becomes procession, fervent slide turns to a spume.
"I'm knackered" at completion,
though, I s'pose I can't complain!
judging by contented beams, the wenches feel the same.
But then they undertake a task, I frankly, find quite odd,
they set about examining by way of nip and prod.
They even size me serpent in assessment of thy thew,
perhaps in awe, I tell them,

"ye should never bite off more,
than ye mouth allows te chew!"

They do not understand me, so I improvise a mime.
It aims to say don't worry, this skin and bone will soon be prime.
The tanned hides come to sudden cease, again we're on the move,
out into dusk comes cook of meat, thy gut gripes its approve.

"Shipmates!".
re-united, with a sprightly air of bliss,
but as he's laid beside us, thy conscience can't dismiss.
Coocoonau!
"how is he?"

[Tonic tests]
"Still feverish.
 He dallies in the deep sleep, he sips but won't take nourish.
 I fear he may be fading, I can do nought but persevere,
 the natives pay him homage, they coat in fruit and scented smear."

"What about Mole?"

"They've buried im! They showed me new dug mound.
 Twas not far from the settled spot
 where the daft bugger drowned."

[How can we call them savage?
They all do nought but watch our hind,
a more attentive catering host I doubt you'd ever find.
Nothings too much trouble. It's too good to conceive.
It's seems they've taken to us.
I just can't see them letting us leave]
"Ahhhhhh",
 the feasts delivered.
A bowl of........... "beetle broth!?"
Some swim, some rigor, mortised,
but complaint might incite due wroth.

I'll eat it cus I'm famished, if I weren't I've have to say, that
"they should have more manners" if they want their guests to stay.
"They've kept the best meat fe themselves!"
 charred sinews fall asunder.
 The chief man chooses finest cuts, then signals pack to plunder.

"Frenzied salivation."
Vultures without wings,
clamber to the carcass for their rabid ravagings.
Can't make out what sort of beast,
headless frames? bout size of man,
judging by the fight for feast their other days are banyan.
I've n'er seen nothing like it,
rampant dog eat dog.
Grapple, scuttle, evade, flee, covet, hounded slog.
It's cage becomes a tug 'o' war which ends with savage snaps,
finally fragmented, the feeble forage for the scraps.
The 'Lady's' men, reflecting on the dumbfounding defile,
ration that it's safe to say,
"Looks like grubs, grub for awhile."

Nightfall brings reunion, assembled defecate,
proceeding to some kind of trance, they get into a right old state!
Trembled drool, chanted fuel, eyeballs out of sight,
ghostly orbs, ringed with daubs, reveal their blood forked white.
Edgy,
as uncertain as,
the moment that we met,
but, no harm is directed,
we're still revered?
as of yet!

Fervour's dissipation dwindles, cortege wreaths adorn,
retirement secludes twitchy night,
deformed shadows jar respite,
but all's as is it was before, come rebirth of the morn.

The ritual gratification progressed on for several weeks,
pampering fascination with the form of our physiques.
Diverse copulation ensured weight gain remains firm,
only down side is the bruises on me banging bags of sperm.
Hogmanay and Tonic revelled in the same pursuits,
whilst other two prefer engagement of more subdued resolutes.
Cripp said he'd partake no more, said actions where disloyal,
said he'd rather turn his hands to more rewarding toil.

"Yer'd rather caress cuts of wood!, has fever made ye mad?
Yer wife's distant horizon, she'll never know that ye wer bad."

"But I'd know!
Besides,
don't worry bout me, e hold e candle, dip its wick.
You have no ties to tug at strings, grab e chance, ram till e wrick.
I've made mistake I'll rectify, by salvaging thy stoat,
I'll turn thy days to better ways of resurrecting hope,
now leave me lone to chisel, so as I can build me boat."

I left him. Couldn't understand, how he curbed urge from below,
the slightest titillation always tingled mine to grow.
If he was age of William, his stance would make more sense,
he should "get it while it's going, a boat ull be no recompense,"
sides, why'd ye want to leave a place which lavishes indulgence.

Daily preened till presentation meant I'd never been so clean,
kneaded oil, to supple joints, then massaged to a sheen,
but even heaven has its hell, and rapture turned to woe.
Coocoonau's departure came to land a severe body blow.
It had been expected, though twas still hard nonetheless,
as at the death he'd surfaced from
the depths of his unconsciousness.
I was not there,
but Tonic said he'd stirred and then took stock,

he had some kind of sudden fit,
sat upright, face was fixed with shock,
he started screaming "mange vous" and frantically he flailed,
some natives helped to pin him down, to repress that which ailed,
they forced liquid for benefit, he fought, but had to sip,
the nourishment had come too late, he tensed,
then life did slip.

"Twas no way te go, fe the picture of a hero."

For he, thou in the clutch of death, chose words he did repeat,
(Tonic mulled that) vous means "you", and mange means to "eat".
Thinking of our vigour, what a kind considerate friend,
selfless, looking out for us
right up until his end.

[Yet again, these natives endear with their stabs to achieve feat,
that night we celebrated life, they even slay a beast for meat,
no simple task! in these here parts, as critters seem so sparse,
I don't recall a sighting since I've idled on me arse]

Further frenzy ensued, which bordered on deranged,
if this course be common, I'd consider going estranged.
However, dwelling with reflect, their greed had happened twice,
so, I intimated that they ought to spare me an odd slice.
You'd o thought I'd asked for arm and leg! the way they carried on,
begrudging grunt, "if looks could kill!", for just a small incision.
I got a piece from Maibalai, a willing wench,
though now averse,
I wondered could she spare it! [masticate] I've sampled worse.
But morsel, be it meagre, retained elements of chaste,
emitting upon swallow, a bitter after taste.

Events took yet another turn, again twas not for best.
Billowing smoke, black as soot, rose bove distant craggy crest.
We took to expedition, a forested foray,
it seemed to me, meander, as if guides had some how gone astray.

Drenched and dehydrated by the dense humidity,
a buzzing mozzy banquet as we battled through topography
till thinning rendered clearing revealed ocean on the other side,
twas then we sank, crest fallen from destruction of our pride.
There! two hundred lengths or more,
disbelief drew pained proclaims,
'The Lady' crackled midst engulf of raged infernal flames.
Twas presumed she had floundered,
now she's back and lost again,
suppressed regression surfaces,
as smoke signals that this will be our permanent domain.
Slow subsidence bathed her through the lap of cooling laves,
resurrection was but fleeting, then she sizzled neath the waves.
"Goodbye old girl."

Solemness effected, but it dwindled within week,
the hedonistic lifestyle ensured mood was briefly bleak.
Cripp laboured isolated,
a fervour fed by guilt,
Crow turned horticultural,
a budding tinged with wilt,
Tonic strove to deter puss,
a foiler of the fester,
Hogmanay can't get enough,
a serial molester,
I had tired of such pursuits, for fancy became pester.
But still incessant fondle weighed, they shagged as if deprived,
thy puff just never seems enough until,
'The Day' arrived.

It began as any other,
a dawn of glinting gold,
twas little to portray events that shortly would unfold.
Thomas Cripp (of all people!) turned out to be a wily dog,
during weeks of seclusion, he'd chosen to befog.

Until, that is, this epoch, when he opted to confide,
slinking under latticed leaves he crept and slid longside.
A hand was placed upon thy mouth, I wakened with a start,
"shhhhh, it's me, don't cause alarm, I've secrets to impart,
but not here, I can't stay long, meet me at Bluff Cove instead,
I beseech, don't change habits, or we all will end up dead.
With that he left as he had came, but I was left to muse,
the baffle of bewilderment of his fleeting effuse.
So I rose and clung to routine, staging scrupulous detail,
when it was safe to do so,
I took portended trail.

The veiled haven proved sterile,
with not a sole in sight,
uneasy still encumbered, then the fireworks did ignite.
Spasm rustled undergrowth,
[administered dull thud]
sent a native sprawling,
his skulls fracture pulsed its blood.
Emerging, Cripp's grip dropped its rock, he did not seek approve,

"the black was in the bushes,
e's tailed e every move.
Just as they've done to us all, since day that we arrived,
good fortunes not the reason as to why it is we've thrived."

His eyes were apprehensive.
Expressions dwelled in searching stares,
twas akin to vexed quarry, seeking sight of that which snares.

"We're being fattened for a feast,
they gorge upon freshly deceased,
what is it do e think happened to Coocoonau and Mole?"
"Tonic said that each were graced, then buried in a hole."

"But tell me, did e see it? did e witness with his eyes?

127

The answers **NO**!, you've all be duped, their manners just a guise."

"Thomas, **THOMAS**, calm yourself, perhaps it is yer overrun,
could be the isolation, or could be length in the sun."

"**We have no time to banter words,**
now two! have been dispatched,
twon't be long for them to find and our conclusion hatched.
I'll prove it, but we must be swift, before they track our taste,
much is done, but still to do, there is no time to waste."

I followed.
Thought I'd placate him, as poor bloke seemed perturbed,
he led me to a clearing,
where the ground had been disturbed,
he knelt and began burrowing,
"hurry Rasmus lend a hand,"
I offered him a hollow hoe, retort to his demand.
Then I struck unyielding bone,
Cripp scurried to reveal,
attributes,
a head, now void had suffered an ordeal.

"Mole!" was desecrated, minus orbs, his tongue, his brains,
then further delve divulged twas all that's left of his remains.
Fear. Realisation. The kind that pounds to constrict chest,
the end that fate had chosen
was just too hard to digest.

"We're gunna die!
we're marooned,
out numbered
but they'll get a scrap",
defiant march soon halted with the advent of back handed slap,

"pull eself together man, at same time, put me down,
tis not the time nor place for reinforcement of renown.

I've built the boat to save us, it awaits us in obscurity,
but there's deeds need to be done
afore we all can put to sea."

Drinkette dropped,
jumped,
thumped the air with an elated swing,
a great weight had been lifted from the load of foreboding.
"Cripp, come ere ye cunning cant,"

"there is no time, so stop e rant,
we must make haste this instant
f'were to make good our escape.
You go find Crow and Tonic,
I'll go and get provisions and I'll see if I can sway the ape.
Meet me at the Loganstone, be swift, be shrewd, truncate,
but should you be discovered. Forgive me, for I shall not wait."

"Farewell".
Separated!
senses coincide to clash,
caution contends with the rampant overwhelming urge to dash.
Anxious, mindful of the time, my mission can't be late,
repulsion, stems with notion that I ate part of me mate.
Elation, interjects, discovered passage from limbo!
fear, embeds its coming cross a horde of smiling foe
ego, not to be outdone, responds, eager to fight,
self, proceeds to input oar, reintroducing flight.

"Damn you, cease ye badgering, yer ranker forces jib,
yer babble subdues charity, the sense to save thy sib."
Cherishing benevolence, to keep the blur at bay,
the way is clear, I find myself on verge of cloaked affray.

Tonic was surrounded!

As usual, Cure was in demand

[alert will cause alarm]
So, craftily I crept,
to his hut, scrawled, hoped twould not be swept,
ciphered whistle, drew departure, leaving Trib's fate in his sands.

Roving with contorting crawl,
I came upon next port of call.
Bugger's hut seemed silent, whilst deceivers go about facade,
but,
drag marks!
trench from shelter,
knife is whipped from its scabbard.

"by God, if they've harmed him!"
they ardour wills me to unleash, rampage, avenge, extract,
[Will's wise words, recall wills whim]
tis all that I can do to pause and refrain from exact.

Simmering recce, surveys tracks on camouflaged pursuit,
I do,
but do not wish to find the extent of their route.
Thy eyes discover [mystyfied]
oblivious, tinkering old fool

"Christ yull be the death of me",
Crow turned to face the ridicule.
"Who's grabbed and rattled yur cage?"
came retort with surprise
"no one, I just thought ye wer dead,"
"what prompted that surmise?"

"The furrows betwixt hut and here. It looked like yud been dragged.
Twas sure that when I reached ye, I ud find that yud been dagged."

"The furrows are from shuffle,
as ye see, I have no legs!
I woke up in fine fettle, found, some filch, had nicked me pegs,
it don't make sense! who'd use um? I mean who'd [interrupt]

"**this is no time fer idle jaw** [features almost fall to floor]
look old friend, I'm sorry, but I have te be abrupt.

We're all in mortal danger,

this declaration is sincere,
no time for preparation,
just come, and let's get out of here."

"**What d'ye mean, I can't just leave!** just look, me seeds,
they're bout te bloom,"

"fer our sakes, keep ye voice down Will, this is no place te boom.
We have te leave this instant, there's no time to explain,
twill be the end fe both of us, should dawdle force remain.
Just trust me,"

"what like Mole did? A lot of good it did fur him.
He followed, did just as ye said,
fur what?
a throttle, on a whim,"

"**IT'S NOT LIKE THAT!**"

"argh, there ye go, the slightest word evokes a rage,"

"look, it was not like that.
As I said,
I found him dead,
I implore ye te believe gage."
Crow eye'd virgin accord.
S'pose it wouldn't hurt to give the benefit of doubt.

A wry smile bridged the divide.
Then [rear of Rasmus] disturbed eye,
reflected to ratify
appearance of a scout.

"Look Rasmus! it's Waywanay", accompanied a wave,
I knew that Will still doubted, so I needed him to pave.

"Call him over"
(as he did, I knelt to clasp grit, watched Will's gaze),
the native ran and raised his spear to pierce the secure glaze.

Reeling release thrashed his face,
the spear head sliced thy shoulder,
fear twould've been the death of me, if I had been much bolder.
Blinded by abrasion, braids were seized and thrust to sand,
squirming suffocation,
the captive fought to force unhand,
with desperate claw, futile fumble,
me bestride to drive submerge,
the little bastard grabbed me sack to generate a wrenching surge,
the clutching clash intensified, but neither would let go.
I rose above the agony,
applied a swift fico.
The purpose ebbed away,
then death came to allay.

Speechless. Crow then cackled,
"Christ, he tried te splice me lice.
Tis lucky both weren't hackled."

"It all has been entice,
they mean te sacrifice,
now jump aboard, I'll have us out of this place in a trice."

Did those bushes rustle?
are they full of pending strife?

Panic provokes hussle,
freedom bears conserving knife.
Was it an accomplice? [lifting Will to piggy back]
or have senses gone amiss?
blighted eyes search for attack.
Every patch of concealment, potential sinister shield,
draws the dart of anxious orbs, foliage fails to yield.
Swiftly into lolloping stride,
"Ahhhh", the wall of weeds is pierced,
bellowed, slashing exide, the pulsed proceed is fierce division.
Swiping, swirls surroundings,
commingled shades of chaffing green,
scythe mows on regardless, willing crimsons intervene.
Desperate tussle forges, frantic, seeks to emanate,
compacted clumps, rooted ridges meld to trip erratic gate,
invaded limbs retaliate to jostle, rip and lash,
encumbrance constricts density to restrain lumbering thrash.

"Steady lad, there's nought behind,
 stay still,
 catch ye breath"

The clinging cripples shrewd words
effaced spectre of impending death.
Kneeling to recover,
anxious respite wheezed,
whilst knowledge sought the cutest course to prevent being seized.
Mists of fear,
dispersed to clear, replacing wits dictate.
Pickle courts contrivance? Circumnavigate!

Stealthily, we cleave contours, meandering duck and skim.
Crow checks the rear,
"the coast is clear" around the hostiles rim.

"There! there!, 'The Loganstone'",
 arrived without cicerone,
 the coveted cove immerses, coruscate is threshed to cool,
 it soothes thy aching ligaments, burden of tropical mule.
 Relief is brief, for

"where is Cripp?"
 there is no sight or sound,
 "pray he's not forsaken us, abandoned, to compound."

There is no boat, there is no Cripp,

"the bastards left us to our doom,
 JUDAS!" is spat at the waves, assistor to the traitor's spoon.

"We're done fe, good as gobbled. But by God they'll get a fight!"
 [then, disturbance distracted the perusal of their plight]

Breaking from the undergrowth, Tonic raced as if possessed,
 could hardly catch his breath from dash
 to expose that which he'd witnessed.

"Hame .... Hamish,"
 "calm down Trib,
 what's the matter? where's the Scot?"

"they've took him....
 put him...
 in a pot,
 they're,"

 twas then came interruption,
 its pitch would taint forthcoming dreams,
 discord, sourced by boiling bubbles, tenderising,
 scalding screams.

"Oh Lord, **please** forgive me.

he would not come,
tried to persuade,
infatuation had evolved with constant serenade.
As I left,
kerfuffle started, grabbed him, dragged him by his hair,
thy transfixed feet were rooted, I could not help, I didn't dare,
it's all my fault!
what could I do?
this poltroon's left him in a stew."

The babble ceased with advent of a firm, but beneficial slap
"I'm sorry,
but tis no one's fault,
we've been caught in tenacious trap.
No one can save poor Hogmanay, we can not save each other,
twon't be long afore their smile, and we succumb te smother."

"Cripp,"

"don't mention miscreant, he's left us high and dry,"
"no, **CRIPP**!"
Crow pointed to the sea, to guide astonished cry.
The chippy beckoned vigorously,
submerged to neck by lapping sea,
[bewilderment afflicted, but enticement drew them in]
resistance strove to subdue,
until lapping waves splashed beneath chin.

"Christ Cripp, what ye doing? Has detach drove ye dim?
 why are we here? where's the boat? are we s'post te swim?
 Trib's strugglin te get this far.
 Carried, Crow is below par,"
"If yull let e get a word in! e future is well faired,
 I'm not just ere to have a dip,
 everything's prepared."

"Where's the boat?"

"Patience Drink, it lies right ere below,
 twas rolled out with the tide last night, tis upturned.
 Weighted. Full of stow.
 Tis where it's frame is to remain till darkness of the fall,
 we'll have to endure overflow, I know that won't enthral."

"Wh?"

"ere take these pegs and pinch e noses,
 take tubes, assume submerged poses,
 tuck e feet beneath the boat to offset sweeping surges,
 do not forget, tis certain death for all thee that emerges."

"What about me? me legs have gone,"

"well use the boat to stand upon,
 besides e all will have to sink with lowering of tide,
 use curve of feat, as transient seat,
 till water leaves e exposed, then there'll be no place to hide."

Splutter replaced utter, Cripp descended out of view,
 the others looked at implements and wandered whether to eschew.

[Whispering.]
"Rasmus I don't like this, without me legs I'm bound te drown,"

"Don't worry Will, if boats too low, I will not let ye down, te flounder.
 Bolster self, alternative, is roasting on their grill,
 this path we take, though not well worn is only one that will fulfil."

[Noses nipped, they slowly slipped and dipped beneath the swell,
 detachment drew diverse reaction from compress of liquid shell]

"This blind confines oppressive.
Thy slippin stumps lack fast purchase,
this is thy first encounter of a damned afflicting cowardice.
But droplets quibble, dribble, gush, their salty plug provokes,
swallowing gasps, wretched retch, exacerbation evokes
a breathless consternation to this task which I'm subjected,
though I darest not surface lest thy thrashing flounder be
detected."

"The four of e, should be enough, te labour, make good thy escape,
   the duskies done e favour, when they ensured fettles ship shape.
These damned fools are contemptible,
   they could not see the wood for trees,
   they're needed in the short term, so for now I shall appease.
The only problems Drinkette, e's mountainous, but also cute,
   shall have to contrive cunning course, a means to mute the brute."

"Well Drink, yer life is never dull.
(This shoulder doesn't half sting!)
This deluge's been an eye opener, can see fer yards,
it's entrancing.
Just keep calm and slowly breath,
ye see!,
ain't so bad,
can't call te mind this kind o fun, since I wer just a lad.
There's fishes darting everywhere,
save effortless who float te gawp,
there's spotted, speckled, spiky, striped,
the flat one's skim above the scaup.
Can see Cripp looking over", [hand signal]
watch this [cheeks balloon],
[stalk's removed, bubbles bobble, former fiend acts like buffoon]

"Tis like I'm living neath the sea,
a new horizon surrounds me,
tis like a new beginning,
a slate wiped of its past.
If only it could have no end,
if only it could last!"

"I never should have left him, [inner guilt reproached]
no man, no matter what his crime, should end up being poached.
OH MY GOD!, poor Coocoonau,
they must have done the same to him,
what kind of savage are they to enact a deed so grim?
White meat!, s'all they've eaten, even
Coocoonau was fair of skin,
they must have acquired taste, **OH CHRIST**!
What about their cherubim?
Tens of them were with child, result of romping with the crew,
they're stock piling the future feasts to fatten for the slew.
MONSTERS, monsters, one and all,
a bigger bad I doubt you'd find
and all done underneath my nose, how could I be so blind?"
[Condemn advanced to tarnish. Berating personal smears.
Releasing grief, aqueous cloak
absorbed poor Tonics tears]

[Claustrophobic hours came and went for those confined.
Immersed, emphasis reversed, waters line declined.
Seated on their saviour, cuffed by curious kelps,
buffeting intensified till surface rippled scalps.
Slight shiver turned to quiver, as the signal came to rise,
ebony and smothered moon ensured constant disguise]

"**Fireflies**!", island is alive,
torches criss cross frantically,
anger fuelled bewilderment,
frenzy sought the flesh that flee.

"Keep e heads down one and all, or silhouettes ull soon betray.
We'll have to wait, till waves abate
or we'll be skittled by the sway."

Nervous vigil ensued as the source for flight receded.
Some turned to God,
some charmed their luck for links to be seceded.

"Finally!" Cripp gave the word,

"well Christ it's about time!
I'm perished cold, me stumps are numb"

"at least e boots ain't full o slime"

"fer our sakes, stop yer quibblin, look lively lads bestead,
ye may be cold, but least yer live, be thankful yer not....."

"get down!"

The whining ceased abruptly.
Some hundred yards along the shore,
"two torches searching spritely, no, three, no, five, no, more."

"Quickly lads, unleash each end,
don't dawdle till we have to fend.
All together,
grip'n'flip, grab the casks, the mast, push off. **The oars**!"
"there in"
"**JUMP IN!,
ROW FOR E LIFE**."

"Cummon lads, put backs to it, and rid us of consuming strife."

The quartet heaved, save for Trib,
who offered semblance of a stroke,
burdened by the butchery and wound of broken yoke [he stood]

"**Murderers, murderers**, one and all, I lavished tender care.
And this is how you repay dedication to your welfare.
I scorn upon your ..... "

"sit down Trib, curb, contain thy rocking roar,
 we're doomed te tip or circle if ye do not grab that oar."

Reluctantly, the rant, resumed his place within the four,
but bluster was as fervent as was degree of implore.
The flames approached, encroached the sea,
furious spears flung vigorously,
sliced sable screen, forcing careen,
but none did strike their aim.
The dripping oars of union stroked further from the maim.

"Heave, ho, heave, ho, heave, ho, heave, ho.
 Well done lads, we've cleared the spears,
 but soon the chase is bout te start,
 twill not be long afore their leaky lean logs will depart.
 We must row as none before,
 strain until we have no more
 and pray our sweat is strong enough te deflate those that chase,
 tonight old Neptune's with us,
 he's shepherding clouds te become shrouds,
 in hope that snuffle blinds te leave us lost without a trace."

The rowing was relentless, skin was chaffed till wore was sore,
exhausting exertions, yet still they mustered more.
Finally they flagged to lay, with reserves at their neap,
fatigue flowed to laden lids and drifted them to sleep.

[Tis with regret, I have to tell, with wakening of morn,
discovery of empty place, left all aboard forlorn.
Trib had gone.

Must be his outlook could not surmount sorrow.
Melancholy moved him to immerse impending morrow.

"Damned fool."

"Such a waste"
of a considerer, most kind,
tis no befitting ending for the man who dwelt behind.

Sail and sore thus occupied the following thirteen days,
ail and bore oppressed us as we charted level maze.

"**Land ahoy**,"
an island! surfaced,

"is it safe?"

"how can e tell?
It still could be a heaven that again is guised by hell.
For this one appears much the same, as one we left afore",

trepidation fills thy gills as distant land becomes the shore.
Distend ogles all that moves on drag of golden marge,
severing stems,
our getaway is cloaked in camouflage.
Tentative, the trio's merge, afflicted nerves with deja vu,
which thrived amongst gnarled foliage, contorted by taboo.
Sprouting boughs amidst shittims,
deviate to stabbing limbs,
the merest snap,
became a trap.

[Is it such, in shadows taint, can nibblers lie lurking?
the answer came with rapid flurry from progressive firking]
  [A bird]

"Jumping Jehosaphat!",
  Cripp leapt like an acrobat,
  Crow clung that much tighter
  and Erasmus clenched his mitts.
[Cacophony erupted, prompting myriad of fleeing flits]

"Christ, the islands come alive,
  there's load of meat fer us te thrive,"
  [and so it was they dined upon whatever they could capture,
  until a chance discovery occurred to end their rapture]
  Exploring shore as yet unknown,
  footprints found
  were not their own,

"**A ship**!",
[instant restraint clasped hold to muffle the Old Codger,
for in his haste he'd failed to spot the rippling Jolly Roger,
"Pirates!"

Shuffle sought seclusion,
scramble parted fusion,
Codger's revolutions saw him land amongst the wiry clumps.

"De ye dump te ridicule,"

"Hey, I'm not yer bloody mule,
  Christ Cripp,
  when ye gunna get around te makin Crow's new stumps?"
"If e gets a broom, I'll bend, so e can shuv it up me arse,
  in case e hadn't noticed,
  me times bin kinda sparse.
  So right now I would be obliged if e ud cease e mutterings,
  so attention can focus on more fruitful happenings.

Look o'er there, along the shore,
two boats moor.
[loud guffaw]
Why is it, those ruffians are celebrating by the score?
Now take a look, there! out to sea,
a third approaches gingerly,
him standing
until landing,
e who barks constant deride.
What's that at his side?
neath emerald, regal, clamlike cloak, what is there to hide?
Has e nidified?"

"I don't know what that be!"
"let them tow and e will see."

[Aboard the boat approaching]
"Damn yu Sham, yu useless ram, yur sweep has gone asunder.
 Match yur mates in rhythmic rates or yull be without plunder."

Bastard Bill surveyed the scene
which sprawled before his unpatched eye,
suspicion's orb worked overtime in readiness to espy.
Cocked ready at his port side, strapped to solitary finger,
was his faithful restless flintlock [An often used harbinger].

"Knucklenose, make ready. Gumgab, thresh the surf,"
tas been a while since I've seen Isle
and set foot pon its tropical turf.
Raising weapon to the sky, impatient prime exploded,
the buoyant rabble ceased their bray as Bill's gofer reloaded.
[a midget, name of Lickit, whose soul was long since sold,
he lived his life neath Bastard's veil and did as he was told]

"Cease yur wail, you poxy hogs"

[Bastard beckoned forth bandogs]

"Urg, Frapp, Nigernatch, (where is he?) Sasquevere
[Robust, ruthless allies, four of five exempt from fleer].

Right then lads, yu know the drill.
[Lowering to huddle]

Leave tat chest here, whilst I ramble,
on return commence the scramble,
whence we sits for final course, twill be us gets te fill.
So keep these serviles appetised!

Frapp, divide, graze haf the flock,
go gather all that we can stock.
Urg, ensure the rest don't flee, we cant afford a mutiny,
[to ear] enact thy decree,
tuther lads, grab tuther chest, tread carefully and come with me."

Clandestine trip had scarce begun, afore it came to abrupt halt,
beside a tranquil teaming pool, where fall secluded vault.
Bide nestled pon dampened rocks, splay absorbed crammed fother.
Attracted insects skim, skirt, hang, zzzub,
"harangue" flails the bother.
[Rustle prompts activity]

"Ahr Shamus, just the man.
Come here te Bill [hook draws ear]
[whispered] here's me plan.
I need a slumbering sentinel, and out of all I've picked thee,
to guard and deter pilferers. So come embrace thy destiny."

Eyes alight with intrigue, but as of yet uncertain.
Bastard led the patsy to behind cascading curtain.
"There!
[Flickers honey haze repelled to reveal ancient chest.]
Go take a look at horde that's stored."
Sham followed the behest.
[seized hinges squealed]

"Tis empty!",
confusion turned to palter.
Infantile bemusement frowned, but Bastard did not falter.
A shot rang out, boom ricocheted, dot pierced betwixt wide eyes.
Bubbles pulsed to trickle blindness, stagger,
etched surprise, recoiled.
Clumsy crumple slumped supine into awaiting crate.
"That should deflect those filchers who embark to desecrate."

Lickit laughed endorsingly. Bastard ridiculed remorse,
the expedition reconvened upon its calculated course.

"Three went in, but two came out!
so tell me, what's that all about?"

"Maybe e was surplus.
Perhaps a dunderhead.
One things almost for sure,
the poor blighter is dead.
But come, don't get distracted, for we need to keep in touch.
We need to know all that there is if we're to achieve clutch."

[So following in footsteps, the trio traced the four.
Passing trips, impaling dips and retarders galore.
With ancient ankylozing
and freshly decomposing,
but though some bones were brimming, he'd concocted plenty more]
Finally we came upon a tree's abundant girth.
In all my days I'd never seen nought such the like upon this earth.
Cept for size its aspect would mean most would disregard.
To our surprise its trunk was but unblemished barked facade.
Which seemed to have no entrance. Till elf was lifted high.
He wriggled into knotted hole, no bigger than me thigh.

No sooner had he entered,
then the large rock which its base supported,
eased away from rooted mould as henchmans haul contorted.

"What a crafty Bastard!
E's sealed the cavity from within,
knowing that no normal man would ever be that thin.
What e adn't reckoned on is from beneath a leafy hood,
someone would see the secret of his lair beneath deserted wood."

The chest was swiftly swallowed,
bark and boulder re-converged
[fastenings were re-fixed] and the pixie re-emerged.
We followed them back to the beach, to verge of lapping ocean,
where the other chest was opened to arouse frantic commotion.
A free for all those present, where
the grabbers gain the spoils.
A secondary booty, just reward for governed toils.

Scramble, scuffled rummaging, melee, flailed array,
consumed
till Bastard signalled end of raucous interplay.
Most had salvaged something,
though there were some picaroons
who'd ended up with nothing,
Bastard tossed them gold doubloons.
"Hurrah fe Bill", [cheers rang out]

"**Down To The Boats**", [oars commenced].

The celebrators slipped away, containing what was sensed.

[**Euphoria**]
erupted upon reaching locus beyond fear,
for exploration could commence now that again
the coast was clear.

Carve betrayed contraption.
Inside, holed rock was wedged with joist,
to all those seeking caption, twas impossible to hoist.
But for a seasoned carpenter who chiselled with the grain,
the route to cracking problem,
was evidently plain.
Angled skim
around rocks rim allowed access to saw.
Its flowing bite without respite, sliced twice,
dispatching stubs to floor.

Undertook endeavour,
with brute force, chock and lever.
Rotated granite obstacle till, chamber lay exposed.
Daylight danced upon the gnarls to reflect that disposed.

Glimmer, glisten, glint, glow, gleam and glitter dazzled eyes.
Rubies, emeralds, sapphired stones.
Diamonds drew drooled tantalise.
A silver sprawl, a golden haul, enticement nourished gluttony,
restraint could curb no longer,
avarice proved the stronger,
plummeting to embrace depths, instinct urged to gut 'n' flee.
Shovel showered sparkle, desire augmented with each spoon,
every prong and orifice was subject to festoon.
Regalia enacted,
vibrant hues refracted,
revelry distracted till emergence of the moon.

Daybreak brought sobriety, a musement to digest.
Exuberance surrounded, not to mention the sealed chest.
[We took a stab at entry. Last night we gave the lock some clout,
we even speckled powder, but still it was too stout.
It must surpass in value, else why would they go to such pains,
surely stash would prove the pluck of Bills ill gotten gains.
We cant afford to leave it, though load may be romance.
We know not of its content, but we have to take the chance]

"Cummon Crow, Drink, shake a leg,"
"I would if I had one!"

"Well while yuv snoozed, I've chipped e pegs,
 the seconds almost done."

"Thank Christ fe that, I thought old git would piggy me till coffin."
Erasmus stood, stared stony faced, then gave a teasing scoff grin.

"Here try these on, they'll hav to do, they're coconut and stale.
 There's knobble on each bottom to prevent e from impale."

"Awrrr Cripp me lad,
 there just the job, these husky cups both fit a treat,
[Will then stood and did a twirl] tis good te be back on me feet."

"Hey Thomas, what ye dun te chest,"

"have secured shaft un wheels.
 Twill help e over bumpy ground, prevent e rocks un reels."

"Who sais it's me te bear the brunt!
 what about you ye skinny runt?"

"Rasmus, put tegether, me and William could not heft.
 Tis only e that has the strength to pull that which we've reft.
 "but wheels are only at one end! What's the good in that?"

148

"Twill be easier to convey than if I had left it flat."

 I'd never seen nought such the like,
 though as I heaved, his words were right.

"So now that e is satisfied and tested secure trunnels,
 I suggest, e gets to scooping, fill e pockets to their gunnels."

Already crammed, it didn't hurt to squeeze a little more.
Stuff accomplished,
came emergence and procession to the shore.

The whining wheels assisted, but it still was fair old weight.
Cripp and Crow though cumbersome both did there best to placate.
Eventually we came upon our intact camouflage.
Bared,
we hoisted booty and commenced launch of the barge.
Grimace, grunt, exertion but that settled would not budge,
twas as if the craft had settled in a mire of sucking sludge.

"She's dug her claws,"
"well get the oars
 and prise,"
"no blast e eyes.
 If they are snapped, then we'll be trapped
 and Bill ull cut e down to size.
 Best go and grab provisions whilst I find some logs to free.
 No Will, e stay, let Rasmus stray, I need e to help me,
 [with urging prompt] I'll whistle when its time to put to sea."

I gave eye of uncertainty, Will gestured reassure.
Twas not he that I pondered,
twas what the chiseller had in store.
Thy shoulder bore the brunt of stern, rotated, disconcerted gaze,
would withering image be the last of them
thy memory would emblaze?

Greed, betrayal, double cross, which deceit would emerge,
I wrestled with uncertainty. Hunted, despite retorting urge.

[Need. Thy scarce emotion when connected to another,
but Will had breached stowed barriers, to become as a brother.
To ne'r set eyes pon lineaments again, within thy span,
would fracture crusted fury of a raging ruffian]
The only brood to comfort me,
was trusting Will implicitly
and whereby once thy distrust would have vented violent rage,
this time I must believe in him, although it seems an age.

[A quaver wafts the lofty leaves and warble does engage]

Quickened pace,
for face to face,
to allay hugger mugger.
Though nerves were fraught,
twas as it ought,
as clearing revealed Bugger.
By God, they'd both been busy,
a row of reels led to the tides,
a brace of secured coconuts dangled below boats curving sides,
but still their puff was not enough,
"come Rasmus lend a hand"

[chucking load] chest was ....reeeeee............lifted,
awaiting prow was shifted,
treasure repositioned,
we propulsed from stagnant strand.

Splosh the surf and jugglenuts, momentum gets away,
catching quoth, frantic froth evolves to tuck and splay.
Cripp was first to reach her,
Will became beseecher,
I looked toward impeacher,
would he condemn to embay?

Wave, waver, wave
extended to a hand,
striving tips, oblivious they'd exorcise gratuitous brand.
Erroneous misgivings, wash away with sterling tugs aboard.
A new illuminating light, accentuates accord.

With buoyancy amended, drip soon dries neath sultry sun,
our virgin voyage of affluence, though unmapped, had begun.
Or so we thought!

We'd scarce had time to weigh up fortunes,
ardour had but tugged a league,
when looming sail, full and flowing, filled us with intrigue.
[that was]
until athwarting ominous bones,
writhed to leave dejected,
to this day, I know not how twas Bastard Bill detected.
But there was his avenging prow,
bearing toward resigned bow,
Crow said "**ROW, ROW FUR YUR LIFE**",
but time knew it had none.
A glimpse of opportunity, had but come and gone.

A sudden "BOOM"
from smoky plume,
Cripp's gesticulations reared.
Warbled, whooshing, turbulent,
his head then disappeared.
Incredulous rigidity, as if uncertain what to do,
remonstration relapsed, seeking spasms did ensue.
The crumpled carcass spurted gore,
drenched allies were left in awe.

A secondary salvo burst, still its purpose remained proud.
The vessel, vile, foreboding, bore down,
to administer that avowed.

She skirted within distance,
her muskets ready to expunge,
[pensive] came the order
fusing with devoted lunge.
William cloaked me to the keel,
sheltering impeding zeal,
a leaden deadly downpour, deluged,
whizzing, thudding, slicing sea,
[the demon dreadnought ran past, then she turned a quarter lea].

Thy dearest laboured, gripped me tight, respired, limped till still.
I knew but did not want to know [lifted]

"Will, [shake] **WILL**."

Vacant, glazed, soulless. Thy grief began to greet.
Tenderly I tilted to allow our eyes to meet.

"Oh Bugger, Bugger, say taint true, tis more than I can bear.
I had not contemplated day when you would not be there."

But spirit had abandoned, outlook pierced to that beyond,
licentious deed, had ripped thy need
and broken enforced bond.

"WHICH WILL NOT BE BROKEN!"
yet extent lay unspoken,
thy chest will brace the billow of these aching swollen sighs,
though there not be canvass large enough to contain leak of eyes.
[caressing close]
"There, there Old Boy, thy roving days are at an end."
[a gentle rock]
a lullaby, to pacify thy friend.

Lapsing lids, I lifted, lowered, executed wish to blend.
Wilting with his hight.
He slowly ebbed from sight.

A shot burst to awaken, it fizzled, passed thy distant ear,
it resurrected senses. Penetrated blear.
Consuming anger swerved thy grief,
it reached, erupted from thy core,
rant'n'rave, stomp'o'wave, grab'n'thrust'o'oar.
Assassins had anchored,
two teeming launches loomed,
again their slay began to spray,
for all,
seemed I was doomed.
But. In fact their slavish lust, which blindingly obsessed,
had overlooked residence of that which I still possessed.
If I was about to die,
then treasured chest would also lie
with me, mongst bones and barnacles that languish on the bed,
thy action would torment those live and benefit those dead.
Mauling, hauling burdening beast until we teetered on the brink,
instantly came cease of fire,
as bad blood curdled with desire
to prevent deprivation and avoid impending sink.

"**Hold it there**,
unknown corsair, consider, don't be eager.
I'm sure we can,
talk man te man,
yur cut will not be meagre."

"**DON'T DARE TE DECEIVE ME!**
I know tongues motivations snide,
a bearer of best interests is what thee'd have implied.
[Bastard's boat drew nearer]
Drag 'n' draw oars,
BACK I SAY.
Take thee but one ripple more
and we'll both be away."

153

Drinkette's angers slavered spume
and blood forked gaze enforced relent,

"Hold there lads,
this blackguards stance tells me his words are meant.
So tell me,
how can I appease?
would yu have me on my knees?
or maybe tis that notion rose, t'we'd share und I'd engraft yer"

Shut yer gob ye murdering squab." [cut compliant laughter]

Discord lurched
"Steady lads,
t'would not be wise te impinge,
tilting scales te our disfavour.
Besides,
this urchins boldness gives me food for thought te savour.
So what'll it be
that gratifies thee.
What will soothe thy ire?"

"Resurrection of thy boon,
that is thy desire."

"That can not be!"

"Then you enact the pirates pact
pon curse'll exact dying breath.
Your sworn edict,
thee'll not inflict
or condemn me te death."

Bastard mulled beguilingly,
deciphering for consequence.
Could he afford,
before his horde, to bend to (biased) congruence?

"Aye.
Tis only fair.
Pon Pirates pact I'll swear,
pon proviso thy pact's unspurned
and that,
thee has thy palms upon is safely returned."

"Aye."

Tentatively, boats encroached till secure was at hand,
uncontested restraint,
unmolested distraint,
but I was at the mercy of this seafaring brigand.

And soon as I was dragged aboard, his tongue began to mock,
hustled, bustled ridicule, till I became the laughing stock.
A hooted, booted jester,
a bound dog mauled by pester,
a butt for smut,
a slut for rut,
a leper, plagued by fester.
an isolated limpet clinging to survivals rock.

Bastard was true to his word, but kept me living by a thread,
t'were times I almost succumbed.
Resolve wished it were dead.
I know not length of duress,
as notches ailed with years.
I learned worth of endeavour,
whilst thy Will deflected fleers.
As novelty waned,
the 'stooge' was chained beside the ballast, bove the keel,
twas in the dripping darkness that thy zeal began to wheel.

Skeletal. Cadaverous.
A shadow of thyself,
the single source that drove me was the success of thy stealth.

[A Circle. Size of extent that thy shackles would allow,
splintered claw, slivered sore.
[concealed] slow but fervent plough,
to create, circumnutate,
beaver, badger, boar and blemish baulk,
a finger deep, till timbers weep,
for fibres grease to caulk]

In time, encumber was released
for interfering menial tasks.
Deck by deck,
I worked thy way whilst intent under guise of masks
permitted scrubbing passage to those chores that aided redress,
I've paid particular dotage to the oars and means of express.

"I can not contain surge."
"Ye must."
"It fills me with delight.
 Retribution is at hand.
 Finale.
 Fulfilling flight!"

"Pull ye self tegether Ras,
 final deeds te be begun.
 There's neither time nor place te rejoice till the duties done."
"No, no. Of course, tis folly te presume that that hatched,
 is yet complete,
 must get a grip,
 until they're all despatched."

Thy strength had reached sufficient,
to rattle bones and stir cull,
so placing prepared powder keg in centre of thy circle.

I poured a winding, deadly stripe upon a barren course,
culminating climb from prime,
thy solitude, hence,
forced recourse.

Sprawled, intoxicated,
selection sought and ceased with Grule,
for pon the leagues of turbulence,
his air had placed least ridicule,
as well as tossing the odd scrap.
[I gently muffled, woke his nap]
"Ugh"

"Shhhhhhhhh, ye must be quiet. Ull yull give thy game away."

Discreet urge and usher brought him over to where escape lay.
Trembling plead, stressed thy need for him to assist lower.
Extant gold, down at heels hold, allured prospective rower.
He agreed,
to decline.
Took the coins and tackled line.
Leaving him to fumble,
I crept up on Cypriot,
the half cut helmsman [lonely soul]
tumbled,
cuffs chain tensed garrotte.
In assent,
boat descended.
Tied, I offered second chance,
Grule's fluctuating eyelids closed,
tottering mumble slumped askance,
to rest upon the floor,
immersed in turgid snore,
sensing satisfaction,
I bothered him no more.

"Look how bright it burns! [brilliant blue suffuses white]
glister entices from plight,
oh how thy redress yearns.
Each surging flare, evolves, so spry,
to fizzle, dwindle dark to die,
just as those bonds I coveted,
their sparkle is no more,
but onward goes their radiant core."

Sudden grasp, drags from deplore.
Gripping flight, skipping flights, haste proceeds to starboard side,
dangled drop, angled hop. Liberty's untied.

"Ye coulda gave a hand Will.

Aw Ras me stumps are sore.
[Erasmus smiled]
alright Old Lad.
Put yer feet up,
whilst I oar."

Even,
were the strokes that flowed,
banter briefly reminisced. Abrupt

"BOOM"

brought port profile,
billowing plumes enshrouded list.
Turmoil,
vented disarrays,
obscure shadows, some ablaze,
launched themselves to dousing depths
with clawing desperate flays.

Hurried hurls, scurried swirls,
as boats were dropped amidst confounder,
missing tholes and prepared holes meant frantic toil did flounder.

Fresh rumble resonated,
its moody churning brood increased.
Insurgence expanded,
buckle ruptured release.
Molten searing furnace blistered,
surging splendour soared, scorched sky.
Fiery streams,
inverse beams,
vengeful dreams condemn deservers,
each now doomed to die.
"An eye fer an eye."

Thy scourge declined,
frizzled, resigned.
Saturation sizzled.
Its singed and smouldering ensign,
slipped,
its malice, now, consigned.
"Ah Will, at last tis over! Our ordeal is no more."

Thy words had barely aired,
when there came laboured splashing from the fore.
An indistinct?
a n'er do well,
I knew not whether nose nor gill.
I grabbed an oar,
to raise it high,
was ready to deliver blow.
But it was Bill!

or semblance of.
Cauterized and reeling, his state though unappealing,
drew no act or feeling as he struggled for his life.

Extending, evil neared.
Tempting that still reared.
Apathy then cleared thy soul of rancour, once so rife.
[I sat whilst] Despair pleaded. Disfigured howl did hound.
Thy stroke rejuvenated till, there was no sight or sound.

"Come grab an oar Old Bugger,
 sidle stumps and sit besides,"
[contented glances exchanged,
in unison they coiled the tides.
A shanty propelled spiral,
which whirled with enterprise,
till aging seams
leaked,
till streams,
engulfed.
They rowed to their demise]

Though death's purely contrasting,
Will is everlasting,
and with, thus comes thy charity.

For I've become the buoy that bolsters,
till such time, purpose prevails.
I'm the crutch against the crests, whipped on by lash of gales.
I'm the guide who grabs though prow,
when beacon's flicker, dwindles, doused.
I'm the urge, upon deaths verge, resuscitating oust.

A physique, forged by furnace,
a man that could now care less,
a fiery unrelenting will, another came to tame.
A parched thirst quenched by ripple,
salvations surge with cripple,
perpetual crutch, absolver of,
thy past unflinching shame.

Vilified

Got no money?
got no food?
can I assume that you'd intrude?
can I assume that you would take
food that's handed on a plate?
Then your no different than the fox
who feasts upon the hens and cocks
who've settled down to meditate,
defecate and incubate.

You see.
The careless farmer, first to abhor,
forgot to shut and bolt the door.
Amnesia has consequence
for chickens that have no defence.
Allowing access to the perch,
leaves poor poultry in the lurch
and so begins the bloody feast,
carnage till all life has ceased.

Come the morning, crack of dawn,
the wife goes to distribute corn,
awoken by the chiming clock
instead of chorus from the cock.
Inside the coop, she can but glare
as carcasses are everywhere.
Some lie neatly, cold as stone,
the rest, ravaged, stripped to the bone.
Cursed, the fox is vilified,
thoughts mutate to vulpicide,
but as to blame and where it lies?

Unfortunate inherent genes
dictate behaviour, this then means
instead of dining on a few,
a fox will taste the whole menu.
So here's a tip to those who farm
and wish to keep their birds from harm.
In future, keep your restaurant closed,
to avoid leaving breasts exposed.

Infant's Lament

I will see you
when the sun shines,
I will see you
when I sing rhymes,
I will see you
in the laughter,
I will see you
ever after.

I will see you
in a warm smile,
I will see you, and when I do I'll
open my arms
wrap them round you,
never let go,
oh how I miss you.

I will see you, when the sun shines, I will see you, when I sing rhymes,

I will see you, in the laugh-ter, I will see you, ev-er af-ter.

I will see you,in a warm smile, I will see you and when I do I'll

op-en my arms, wrap them round you, ne-ver let go, oh how I miss you.

Befitting is this end

Tears that overflow to fall whilst celebrating birth.
Uncontrollable outbursts of debilitating mirth.
A thought which manifests into excited overwhelming urge.
Anticipation's tingle as it teeters on eventful verge.
Inner strength to conquer that,
which once you thought you'd fail.
The gift of life extended to the ailing or the frail.
Sensations surge from lips immersed in grip of loves commencing kiss.
Abandoned acts which culminate in wholesome
or forbidden bliss.
Initial unassisted stride,
unstabilised releasing ride,
an overwhelming rush of pride,
first escapade to the sea side.
Adventuring exploration into realms of the unknown.
That substance you had sought for so long
finally becomes your own.
Drifting captivation, consumed within a transient dream
and bathing in the glory of bestowed, cherished esteem.
Then that moment when your baby generates a recognising smile.
These
and all that you hold dear,
occur throughout recurring years,
but in their combinations,
through life's trials and tribulations,
our evolving celebrations
link,
to make this life worthwhile.

The Cuddlehog

A solitary violin intro proceeded with violins, accordion, bottles and tubs.

Doodle da da doodle da da dum dum dum

doodle da da doodle da da dum dum dum

doodle da da doodle da da dum dum dee

dee dum dum doodle da da dum dum dee.

Last line of tune

dee dum dum diddle eye dow.

Accordion accompaniment

Bear bear um pa um pa

Bear bear um pa um pa

bear bear um pa pa bear bum bum bum bum

164

"Are you still here?

Well come along then, don't dawdle, it's closing time!

I haven't got all day ye know, and I, unlike you, have got a home to go to. Oh I can just see it now. The dog ull be slavering to a froth, the damned mutt's had more dinners than I have, and look, go on, look at this ear, chewed, niggled and nagged that much it's started to turn in on itself, can ye see it? Even the wax is afraid to surface. No it's the same thing every night, not to mention me lumbago's playing up again, cor it doesn't arf give me some jip, tis a wonder I'm here at all, what with that and me arthritic gout. Me feet, OH ME FEET, perished cold they are, like ice blocks, I blame this bloody global warming, they've never been the same since the ice caps started melting. Come along keep up, ye wouldn't be going that slow if I told ye the winning lottery ticket was at the end of this corridor, would ye?

Right then, I need to finish me rounds, so listen carefully you need to follow this passageway to its end, then go down the first flight of steps and you'll come to a door with WAY OUT written on it, ignore that, it's the old back door. Turn left, then first right, go through the old snakehouse, there shouldn't be too many of them left now, if there is, the old snake charmers cupboard with his equipment, is behind the viper pit, it was all put in there after he died through lack of antidote. When ye get. Look will ye kindly not interrupt, I need to finish. As I was saying, when you get to the end, go through the sealed doors into the apery, do not follow the exit signs, some little monkey has swapped the signs around. Right, I'll have to get going, oow there goes my sciatica again, that herbal hippo dung isn't working, I thought it was too good to be true, it smelt a bit iffy at the time, should never have bought it from that travelling salesman, it's started me fungal rash itchin again. I tell ye, me spots are as raw as Chlamydia's crotch, so they are, what on earth will be next?